Modern France: A Very Short Introduction

VERY SHORT INTRODUCTIONS are for anyone wanting a stimulating and accessible way in to a new subject. They are written by experts, and have been published in more than 25 languages worldwide.

The series began in 1995, and now represents a wide variety of topics in history, philosophy, religion, science, and the humanities. The VSI library now contains 300 volumes—a Very Short Introduction to everything from ancient Egypt and Indian philosophy to conceptual art and cosmology—and will continue to grow in a variety of disciplines.

Very Short Introductions available now:

ADVERTISING Winston Fletcher
AFRICAN HISTORY
   John Parker and Richard Rathbone
AGNOSTICISM Robin Le Poidevin
AMERICAN IMMIGRATION
   David A. Gerber
AMERICAN POLITICAL PARTIES
   AND ELECTIONS L. Sandy Maisel
THE AMERICAN PRESIDENCY
   Charles O. Jones
ANARCHISM Colin Ward
ANCIENT EGYPT Ian Shaw
ANCIENT GREECE Paul Cartledge
ANCIENT PHILOSOPHY Julia Annas
ANCIENT WARFARE
   Harry Sidebottom
ANGELS David Albert Jones
ANGLICANISM Mark Chapman
THE ANGLO-SAXON AGE John Blair
ANIMAL RIGHTS David DeGrazia
ANTISEMITISM Steven Beller
THE APOCRYPHAL GOSPELS
   Paul Foster
ARCHAEOLOGY Paul Bahn
ARCHITECTURE Andrew Ballantyne
ARISTOCRACY William Doyle
ARISTOTLE Jonathan Barnes
ART HISTORY Dana Arnold
ART THEORY Cynthia Freeland
ATHEISM Julian Baggini
AUGUSTINE Henry Chadwick
AUTISM Uta Frith
BARTHES Jonathan Culler
BEAUTY Roger Scruton

BESTSELLERS John Sutherland
THE BIBLE John Riches
BIBLICAL ARCHAEOLOGY Eric H. Cline
BIOGRAPHY Hermione Lee
THE BLUES Elijah Wald
THE BOOK OF MORMON
   Terryl Givens
THE BRAIN Michael O'Shea
BRITISH POLITICS Anthony Wright
BUDDHA Michael Carrithers
BUDDHISM Damien Keown
BUDDHIST ETHICS Damien Keown
CANCER Nicholas James
CAPITALISM James Fulcher
CATHOLICISM Gerald O'Collins
THE CELL
   Terence Allen and Graham Cowling
THE CELTS Barry Cunliffe
CHAOS Leonard Smith
CHILDREN'S LITERATURE
   Kimberley Reynolds
CHOICE THEORY Michael Allingham
CHRISTIAN ART Beth Williamson
CHRISTIAN ETHICS D. Stephen Long
CHRISTIANITY Linda Woodhead
CITIZENSHIP Richard Bellamy
CLASSICAL MYTHOLOGY
   Helen Morales
CLASSICS
   Mary Beard and John Henderson
CLAUSEWITZ Michael Howard
THE COLD WAR Robert McMahon
COMMUNISM Leslie Holmes
CONSCIENCE Paul Strohm

Available soon:

REALITY Jan Westerhoff
THE ANIMAL KINGDOM
    Peter Holland
THE COMPUTER Darrel Ince

COLONIAL LATIN AMERICAN
    LITERATURE Rolena Adorno
SLEEP Steven W. Lockley and
    Russell G. Foster

For more information visit our web site
www.oup.co.uk/general/vsi/

Vanessa R. Schwartz

MODERN FRANCE

A Very Short Introduction

OXFORD
UNIVERSITY PRESS

OXFORD
UNIVERSITY PRESS

Oxford University Press, Inc., publishes works that further
Oxford University's objective of excellence
in research, scholarship, and education.

Oxford New York

Auckland Cape Town Dar es Salaam Hong Kong Karachi
Kuala Lumpur Madrid Melbourne Mexico City Nairobi
New Delhi Shanghai Taipei Toronto

With offices in

Argentina Austria Brazil Chile Czech Republic France Greece
Guatemala Hungary Italy Japan Poland Portugal Singapore
South Korea Switzerland Thailand Turkey Ukraine Vietnam

Copyright © 2011 by Oxford University Press

Published by Oxford University Press, Inc.
198 Madison Avenue, New York, NY 10016

www.oup.com

Oxford is a registered trademark of Oxford University Press

Library of Congress Cataloging-in-Publication Data
Schwartz, Vanessa R.
Modern France : a very short introduction / Vanessa R. Schwartz.
p.   cm.
Includes bibliographical references and index.
ISBN 978-0-19-538941-8 (pbk.)
1. France—History. 2. France—Civilization.
3. National characteristics, French. I. Title.
DC110.S34 2011
944—dc22
2011007311

1 3 5 7 9 8 6 4 2
Printed in Great Britain
by Ashford Colour Press Ltd., Gosport, Hants.
on acid-free paper

In memory of Susanna Barrows
Beloved teacher and devoted Francophile

Acknowledgments

A lifetime of learning about France in the classroom and in countless trips there inspired this project. I have more French and history teachers to thank than there is room for, but I especially acknowledge the Fleming School's visionary founder, Douce Fleming Correa. Their lessons shaped my life. I would like to thank those who read this manuscript: Elinor Accampo, Mark Braude, Leo Charney, Sarah Farmer, Lynn Hunt, Anca Lasc, and Jon Wiener. They have made this book better, and I am grateful for that and for their friendship. Finally, I thank my family, whose love is my greatest joy and who have joined me in making France part of their lives.

At Oxford University Press, I thank my sharp and able editor, Nancy Toff, and the anonymous readers of the manuscript.

Contents

List of illustrations

Introduction

A fruitful way to consider a nation's history is to observe how it is commemorated at telling moments and key anniversaries. The bicentennial of the French Revolution in 1789 offers an important vision of modern France. The traditional morning military parade down the Champs Elysées (only France and North Korea still mark their national holidays with this kind of martial fanfare) displayed the country's vast array of weapons and soldiers, cutting an attractive figure in their medal-encrusted jackets, feathered helmets, and black boots. The culminating event, however, took place down the same avenue later that night. The twenty-million-dollar "opera-parade" the night of July 14, 1989, unfurled under the rapt attention of a crowd of thousands packed onto the sidewalks and hundreds of millions around the world who watched the simultaneous telecast. Crowds this large had two hundred years earlier shaped the course of history by taking to the streets and toppling the monarchy. Now they remembered, with joyful exuberance, those who made the history that has made French history so central to the developments of the modern world.

The minister of culture, Jack Lang, had hired neither a historian nor a civil servant to direct the spectacle but rather the television adman and stylist Jean-Paul Goude, son of a French father and an American mother, whose relationship with Grace Jones, the

1

Jamaican American singer, reflected his transatlantic flair. Goude dubbed it "La Marseillaise" (the name of the French national anthem), a "presentation of the Revolution in all its states." Rather than retell the story of the French Revolution, the parade staked out the perhaps overstated ground of representing the world and its people, as if the French Revolution might be rethought as a latter-day "Big Bang." More than seven thousand participants from around the world, an enormous re-creation of a steam train, and even a mobile ice rink paraded that night from the Arc de Triomphe to the Place de la Concorde (where once the scaffold stood, ending the lives of hundreds a day at the Revolution's height, including the king of France).

The parade began with a twenty-six-foot-high red Chinese drum, surrounded by 150 Chinese students walking their bicycles, holding a banner that read, "We Continue." The leading marchers of this group were bare-chested and had the words "Liberty, Equality, and Fraternity" emblazoned on their chests in Chinese characters. Only two months after the events of Tiananmen Square in which possibly thousands were massacred by the government, the parade's opening sent the message loud and clear: the French Revolution continued to inspire the course of world history. The Chinese students were followed by more than three hundred drummers, wrapped in tricolor scarves, representing the municipalities of France; and another thousand French drummers dressed in black, with tricolor flags on their backs, faces dramatically lit with small lamps. Another thousand musicians followed, playing traditional French music and dressed in regional costumes.

The parade focused on two themes: the world's major revolutionary cultures and a peculiarly Franco-centric idea of the world (represented mostly by African musicians—especially the celebrated Senegalese drummer Doudou N'Diaye Rose who, dressed as a European conductor, stood atop an enormous float of tam-tam drummers and oversaw African women dancing in tutus

2

reinterpreting "Swan Lake" and surrounded by 450 Senegalese soldiers). Wally Badarou, a Parisian-born composer of African (Benin) descent, served as the event's musical director. To represent the mixing of world cultures, giant spinning women held children of all races and colors, accompanied by turning globes. On the eve of Perestroika and only months after the fall of the Berlin Wall, England, Russia, and the United States also marched in recognition of their connection to world revolution. The parade laid bare a vision of French-led universal world democracy.

The parade's apotheosis took place at the Place de la Concorde where an enormous bandstand of French dignitaries and such world leaders as George Bush, Margaret Thatcher, Benazir Bhutto, and Rajiv Gandhi watched the spectacle. A choir of six hundred French singers performed a "prelude" written by Badarou. Then, raised onto a platform at the base of the Egyptian obelisk, Jessye Norman, the African American opera singer, emerged, delivered by a hydraulic lift cut into the floor, dramatically draped in a tricolor satin robe to sing the French national anthem as the incarnation of the "voice of the world," as Goude would explain.

Although the parade received mixed reviews at the time, mostly for its gigantism, perceived neocolonialism, and lack of narrative, it is a remarkably keen representation and interpretation of the significance of the French Revolution and its foundational role in French and, for that matter, world history. From the opening moments dedicated to China to an American woman of African descent singing the French national anthem, and the spectacle's array of nationalities and cultures in between, it is fair to say that this was a singularly peculiar brand of patriotic celebration. Imagine your own nation giving over its national anthem to a foreign voice in a moment in its history as significant as a bicentennial celebration. The parade defined the transition to "modern" France as a global moment. When the Revolution destroyed the French monarchy it made French people into citizens of the planet as much as of their own nation.

As the Eurocentric view of the world begins to recede, France might seem a quaint and old-fashioned subject driven by nostalgia, scented with a strong perfume of faded glory, and imagined in a picture of tattered tricolor flags. Yet modern France is a subject of great importance at the dawn of our newly defined global era. This volume introduces a younger generation of readers to France while reintroducing it to those who think they know it well. In the mid-twentieth century, such an introduction would have been a narrative of the nation's dramatic political history. This volume integrates that narrative yet foregrounds the dynamism of French society and culture. It presents France's nationalism as highly relevant because it has been framed in a way that tethers the nation's history to that of the rest of the world. The radical changes of the French Revolution defined the "modern" in France as a moment in time, but one with spatial implications: modern France became both a world stage and a cultural crossroads. As a result, France continues to play a role as an essential actor in the development of world history.

French national identity since the Revolution of 1789 has been at once strongly defined by its specificity while also being conceived as having values that could and even should be lived out on a global scale. This rare quality has contributed to France's importance since the nineteenth century, when imperialism and capitalism provoked peoples and nations to collide and communicate on an unprecedented scale. On the one hand, French people have a rich sense of the value of their history and an almost obsessive attention to the nation as a physical place. These are, of course, classic qualities associated with the formation of modern national identity in many places. On the other hand, France has reinforced its significant place in the world by managing the complex forces of spreading their culture around the globe while seemingly magnetically attracting visitors from near and far to visit France (more people still visit France than anywhere else in the world).

While military and economic power played a vital part in France's identity since the Revolution, more than its fair share of defeat and stagnation has counterbalanced such relative strength. France also benefitted from its national investment in new modes of communication and in technologies of transport that helped define the rise of travel and tourism worldwide. This gave the French emphasis on cultural influence a sort of prescience that has both shaped and led to continued world significance. As a result, the French language is spoken far and wide from the Americas to Africa, East Asia, Polynesia, and the Caribbean.

Lest notions of cultural dissemination be understood solely as a remnant of France's own imperial past, French influence and cultural know-how remains alive and well in the heart of other rapidly transforming societies. China, for example, celebrated "the year of France" in 2004, inaugurated by the conceptual artist Daniel Buren's 230 blue flags adorning the main walkway of Beijing's Temple of Heaven. French fashion continues to dominate haute couture around the world. At the same time, French people are at the forefront of international "style" and architecture, which was as true in the first half of the century (consider Art Deco) as it is today. French engineers continue to steer important innovations such as the Airbus. The European company headquartered in Toulouse is the only real rival to Boeing, the American aviation manufacturer. A Frenchman, Paul Andreu, is one of the world's master airport architects—one of the twentieth century's signal international building forms. He designed Roissy–Charles de Gaulle in Paris and has subsequently built airports in Cairo, Shanghai, Jakarta, Bangkok, and Athens, among other cities.

The way "frenchness" has stood for the specificity of something linked to a place and a people—but with global and universal aspirations—remains one of the most compelling qualities of modern French history, and this is nowhere better revealed than in examining Paris, which the philosopher Walter Benjamin went so far as to label "the capital of the nineteenth century." Any account of modern France as a crossroads thus has to account for the remarkable influence of the city. When visitors go to Paris, they are seeking a world capital as well as a national one. The city houses the world's most revered art museum (the Louvre), but Paris has long stood for more than the great works of high European classical culture. It also serves as headquarters to many multinational corporations, and was selected by the Disney Corporation as the location for its theme park instead of sunny Spain because the city symbolized international territory better than any other place in Europe. Disney originally named the park "Euro Disney" but decided that Disneyland Paris had wider appeal. Although France has produced such well-regarded novelists as Honoré de Balzac, Gustave Flaubert, and Marcel Proust, a French author, Jules Verne, is also one of the most translated in the world. This nineteenth-century provincial Frenchman is not read as a French author per se but because of the universalism of his vision of progress and for his prophetic articulation of a planetary consciousness embodied in such classics as *Around the World in Eighty Days*.

If French people and their culture are at work around the globe, if Paris inspires as the vision par excellence of an international capital, the marvel of France is that it still manages to attract visitors from all over the world seeking out the specificity of its artisanal cheeses and the renowned wines grown in its soil, and the drama of its historic castles and significant battlefields. The particularity of France resides in a complex modern national self-definition ruled by the idea and ideal of universalism in culture. This contrasts admirably with the ethnocentric nationalism that emerged across Europe in the nineteenth and twentieth centuries and with the parochialism of American isolationism and subsequent imperialism. As a result, French ideas, values, and culture will remain at the forefront in the global mix of the twenty-first century and beyond.

This book is an interpretive introductory essay rather than a "short history" in chronological order. It argues that French history reveals that the French are skilled at holding contradictory notions in productive tension. France embraced egalitarianism in the Enlightenment and the Revolution and then built an empire in its name. The nation has a tradition of democracy and a sexist and racist one as well. Loyalty to tradition and artisanal expertise is counterbalanced by the embrace of a complex technocracy, which is run with cutting-edge information and military technology and equipment. Everything revolves around Paris, yet French people and visitors profess an undying love of a seemingly timeless beauty that fans out to every physical corner of the nation. These contradictions that in other places might seem like mere hypocrisy do not seem so in France. This is an unusual perspective in a black-and-white, red-state and blue-state world. This embrace of contradiction held in productive tension is an instructive quality in a world as complex and connected as the one in which we live. In that way, France continues to be important as an object of study and as a coherent voice in world affairs.

The echo of the Revolution of 1789 still sounds not simply in glorious commemorations such as the bicentennial parade but also in an ongoing civic discussion that invokes the meaning "the Republic" has had in shaping modern France. This suggests the combined fragility and idealism of democratic Republics. The history of the French Revolution, which established the nation's global mission in the modern era, has not been forgotten in France but has worked as a specter haunting all subsequent political life and historical consciousness in its wake.

Politics alone, however, cannot explain the French nation in modern times. The twin engines of cultural dissemination and magnetic appeal, which have pre-Revolutionary origins but which took on important dimensions in the period after the Revolution, guaranteed that France took its role to be played on a global stage. The French language stood at the center of a project of cultural dissemination often referred to as the *mission civilisatrice* (civilizing mission). In addition to the rich emphasis on the word in France, a powerful and rich visual culture helped establish Paris as the world's greatest host. Francophilia emerged on a grand scale in the nineteenth century. Even French-bashing, usually reserved for traditional rivals such as Britain and Germany, has recently found more global purchase as part of the critique of Eurocentrism. American multiculturalism has made all the former colonial powers open to legitimate critique for past wrongs.

If French language, literature, and visual culture defined a certain form of "frenchness," French ideas of nationality, citizenship, and culture also underwent a fundamental set of transformations, especially in response to unprecedented migrations within France, Europe, and eventually across the world. The Revolution's successful upending of the Old Regime established new nationality laws. Under the monarchy, laws had tied an individual's nationality to the territory in which one was born. In a rejection of such monarchical law, the revolution affirmed nationality through birth. One was French if born of a French father, no matter where you lived. Yet the story developed into an intricate flip-flopping around nationality, which has inflected what it means to be French in a country as marked by immigration as the United States.

The Revolution sought to make the world anew and was forward-looking in orientation. Inspired by the Enlightenment that came before it, on the one hand, and the problem-solving necessity of military global expansion on the other hand, both science and technology became part of the Republican tradition. Napoleon, for example, took an enormous academic team with him to Egypt in a military campaign that also resulted in some of the greatest discoveries of Egyptology, including the Rosetta stone. This prized object was eventually lost to the British but decoded, finally, in 1822 by the Frenchman Champollion. The same revolutionary government founded in 1794 what has become the premier engineering school in France, the Ecole Polytechnique. Napoleon put it directly under the military and gave it the motto *Pour la Patrie, les sciences et la gloire* (For the fatherland, science, and glory). In fact, when the Republic celebrated the Revolution's first centennial, engineering provided the major symbol of the 1889 Exposition: the tower that would eventually bear the name of its engineer-designer, Eiffel, became the world's tallest human-built structure.

One of the accomplishments of the Republic has been the French public educational system. With history and geography nestled at its core, a small book by the historian and educator Ernest Lavisse, the *Petit Lavisse* (1884), taught many lessons to generations of French-educated people and in the French schools that opened around the world in the nineteenth and twentieth centuries. No lesson probably sums up modern France as well as this one: "France, since the Revolution, has spread the ideas of justice and humanity throughout the world. France is the most just, most free, most humane of countries." Despite what may ring as antiquated chauvinism and jingoism, the world has certainly benefitted from this French commitment to and sense of global concern for justice and humanity, in examples that stretch from the unleashing of the Haitian revolution to the United Nations' 1948 Declaration of Human Rights. These ideas of justice were not just spread but also imposed. Yet, as an ideal, universal democracy at a planetary scale is a value worth upholding. If the French Revolution has long been considered a turning point in world history, it may well be because the French, back in the eighteenth century, could envision acting in the name of the rights of people they would never actually know.

The Bicentennial's parade began with Chinese marchers to acknowledge that the Revolution is not yet over. But because revolutionary ideals are hard to uphold, and doing so requires the participation of the entire planet, the course of modern French history has not been smooth. That is also why it provides a story worth telling.

Chapter 1
The French Revolution, politics, and the modern nation

The French Revolution did more than topple a political regime that had continuously functioned for almost eight hundred years. In the process, it created a new political vocabulary and also set the terms in democratic political culture for what would be defined as "modern." French political life and national consciousness ever since have operated in the long shadow cast by the Revolution. It produced a rupture in French political history that has made it a potent "origin," a debated touchstone in relation to subsequent political change in France, and provided a heightened sense of historical consciousness because of the scale of the changes produced by the event. If such terms as the political uses of "right" and "left," ideals of universal education, religious tolerance and democratic participation by a responsible citizenry, and state terror and military authoritarianism in the name of the people are part of the legacy of the French Revolution worldwide, it is not merely a reflection of broader structural change that happened in many places subsequently. Modern French history became a form of "world history" not simply because other places have modeled change inspired by the French Revolution (Mexico, Bolivia, Russia, and China, to name a few) but also because they have done so precisely because the Revolution's vision was universal rather than simply national, aimed at global change and liberation in France.

In the late eighteenth century—an era of revolutionary upheaval—France was not alone. Between 1787 and 1789, revolts in the Dutch Republic, the Austrian Netherlands, and Poland also erupted in the name of liberty and equality. The United States, aided by French money and troops, had only recently declared its own independence from its mother country, England. But what made the French case so compelling was not simply that France was the most populous European state but also the wealthiest, a status on display day and night at the court in Versailles, alight with fireworks and glittering festivities hosted by the young queen, Austrian-born Marie Antoinette. The magnificent fountains at Versailles, complete with gilded statues of the king as Apollo, would soon stop flowing as the monarchy and its opulence came crashing to a halt.

The French Revolution, in word and symbol, added the fundamental concept of fraternity to notions of liberty and equality as it defined its Republic, and created a web of connections that helped solidify the modern nation and its role in a global context. To establish a legacy as powerful as that of the French Revolution, at least two things are necessary: a very significant message, and a flair for delivering it. In the period that the writer Chateaubriand called the quarter century that equaled many centuries, France had both. With a remarkable penchant for taking words seriously and with a dedication to symbolism rivaled by few and copied by many, the French Revolutionaries left an indelible mark. But like any story of political change, it erupted from a set of unfolding and unplanned events.

In the tempestuous summer of 1789, the relation between people and king in France changed. The overall economic health of the nation hovered in near crisis by virtue of a failure to reform the tax-collection system. French support for the American insurgents helped empty the state coffers, and a poor harvest in 1788 resulted in a food shortage in a kingdom used to relative abundance. The appeals for help from the king to the citizenry eventually transformed into complaints against him. Unable to solve the problem of the debt on his own, the king had earlier tried to reform the state by hand picking a group called the Assembly of Notables. They refused to help. Instead they demanded that the king call the consultative body known as the Estates General, which had not met for 175 years. Although that body represented the feudal social order of estates (the clergy: first estate; the nobility: second, and everyone else: third), it would, by the summer of 1789, morph into the body calling itself the National Assembly. By taking an oath on a tennis court when locked out of their regular meeting place, they swore they would not disband until they found the words to proclaim their authority by writing a constitution.

Other important official declarations soon followed, such as the abolition of the feudal regime in a night of deliriously enlightened self-abnegation when the deputies gave up their feudal privileges such as tax exemptions and seignorial dues. Serfdom was thus ended for those peasants still tied to the land, and equality of opportunity, talent, and merit, rather than birth, would henceforth determine one's work and rank. This meritocracy would soon have a flamboyant example in the person of Napoleon Bonaparte, who also thrived on creating institutions and symbols. But first they needed the words.

Toward the end of August 1789, the deputies composed the preamble to their constitution, the Declaration of the Rights of Man and Citizen. Inspired by the American Declaration of Independence, the French document proclaimed, "Men are born and remain free and equal in rights." This statement had enormous ramifications for the social order beyond ending feudalism in thought and deed. If men were born free, how could France justify the system of slaveholding, which prevailed in the Caribbean's wealthiest colony, Saint Domingue?

Many financially motivated Frenchmen attempted to rationalize this hypocrisy and continue slavery, but circumstances prevailed.

A slave rebellion, the promise by revolutionary representatives to extend equal rights to free blacks (rather than end slavery), and the intervention by the British and the Spanish on behalf of white slave-owning planters against the Revolution, turned into chaos in the colony. The French Revolutionaries eventually offered black slaves freedom if they would join forces with the Revolution. Republican commissioners sent from Paris abolished slavery and then informed the government back in Paris, where the deputies in the Assembly subsequently officially voted to abolish slavery in 1794 (only to have it reestablished by Napoleon in 1802). Eventually Saint Domingue's slave population, in a state of constant revolt from the beginning of the Revolution, established the first independent former slave colony in the Western Hemisphere, known since 1804 as the Republic of Haiti. Slavery would be finally and permanently abolished in France in 1848 upon the declaration of the Second Republic.

The question of applying the Declaration of the Rights of Man to half of the population, namely women, was also debated during the Revolution, but the results were far more mixed. On the one hand, women's political activity exploded during the Revolution. They forced the course of the revolution to the Left when, in October 1789, they marched on Versailles and demanded the royal family return to Paris. Many outspoken supporters of women's rights, both female (Olympe de Gouges) and male (Condorcet), met untimely deaths as "enemies of the Revolution." Although women in France would wait a remarkably long time for the most fundamental of rights, including the vote (granted only in 1944), feminist connections to claims for human rights emerged at the start of the modern era in France.

The young noble and friend of General Lafayette, Mathieu, the Duke de Montmorency, who had fought in the American war, exclaimed about the Declaration, "Let us follow the example of the United States: they have set a great example in the new hemisphere; let us give one to the universe." Consider the painting of the Declaration itself by Jean-Jacques Barbier in 1789. In the center, the eye and triangle refer to the Supreme Being, an Enlightenment version of God, overseeing the presentation of these new commandments, displayed as if on stone tablets and heralded by a winged spirit, her arm bearing a torch of enlightenment. On the other side, the allegorical image of France herself, incarnated as Liberty, breaks the chains of the slavery of the old regime. This image, echoing the language of the Declaration, offers up the document's universalizing concepts as a gift for any and all to receive—so long as one actively desires to break free. The Declaration of the Rights of Man and Citizen also proclaimed freedom of the press and of religion, equality in taxation, and equality before the law.

The Revolution thus wrought fundamental changes to the long-standing French way of life. Whereas the American colonists had broken free from England, the challenge of the French Revolution was to reorder society from within. If the Revolution could succeed in France, its supporters also held firmly to the notion that it should, could, and would succeed everywhere. Thus, simplifying the meaning of the Revolution became part of its fundamental conceptualization, hence the importance in having a slogan: "Liberty, Equality, and Fraternity."

What became the most well-known revolutionary turn of phrase was not born all at once. In particular, the concept "fraternity" trailed behind the twin concepts of liberty and equality until the monarchy ended. And, yet, this was the most original element of the founding words associated with the Revolution. The meaning of "fraternity" took hold during the course of the Revolution. The social order would be newly constituted horizontally, among equal men, with brotherhood replacing the paternal bonds that had governed the feudal order between king and people. The revolutionaries believed that this bond of fraternity necessarily extended beyond France to the brotherhood of mankind. With the great fervor of their conviction, they would bring their message to

1. This 1789 painting of the Declaration of the Rights of Man and Citizen is replete with symbols of Enlightenment, such as the eye and broken chains, and reproduces the complete text, engraved on stone tablets.

still-shackled peoples of Old Regimes in the form of war waged in the name of their principles and against Old Regimes throughout Europe and into North Africa.

Adherents to the Revolution also employed new kinds of linguistic address, replacing former hierarchical forms of speech, such as Monsieur and Madame, with "citizen" in the masculine and feminine forms. Parents now named children in honor of the heroes from the earlier era of democratic culture, the Roman Republic, such as Brutus, instead of Roman Catholic saints such as Paul and Jean. This change in names was no mere fashion but part of a much broader wholesale attack on the Catholic Church, Christianity, and the symbolic order on which the Old Regime rested.

Symbols

How did the French revolutionaries manage to be successful in turning words into actions? With the foundational vocabulary to guide it, the Revolution was bolstered enormously by a rich program of symbols that helped give abstract words the concrete sentiments required for widespread adherence. The success of the French Revolution's new Republic resided not only in having overthrown the king (who was eventually tried for high treason in 1792 and beheaded in 1793; the queen, Marie Antoinette, also known as "the Austrian bitch," would follow later in the year) but also in having identified meaningful abstract concepts in such terms as liberty, equality, and fraternity. The Revolution penetrated every aspect of public and private life: it would embody and reflect these new social principles in order to create the very bonds between people that the Revolution proclaimed. The slogan itself, the revolutionary colors, and the allegorical figure of Liberty were emblazoned on everything from playing cards to chamber pots. Sartorial allegiance to the revolution included the tricolor cockade, a small badge of blue, white, and red ribbons worn on one's clothing, designed in 1789 to combine

17

the white color of the monarch with the red and blue of the city of Paris. In addition was an assortment of sashes, feathered tricolor-banded hats, and more natural hairstyles that rejected the fashion among the wealthy for wearing wigs, all of which were used as means to garner civilian loyalty. Dress so shaped identity that the Revolution's most radical element became known by their code of dress. The working classes who embraced the Revolution became known as the "sans-culottes"—those who wore long pants instead of knee breeches.

Under Napoleon, symbols continued to multiply. The generals of the French Army wore more plumes, medals, and ornate gilded jackets than ever before; Napoleon introduced the golden eagles on flagstaffs whose protection in battle was as important as the regiment's living members. As vital to each soldier as his musket was his tricolor cockade. The revolutionary government adopted the tricolor as the official national flag in 1794.

The citizen-army, the first built through a universal draft, was effectively transformed into functional troops because they were given something around which to rally. In the same way that for centuries the Roman Catholic Church and the monarchy had offered a rich culture of symbols and rites, the army rituals were part of the canny work of the revolutionaries who understood what might be thought of as the power of advertising to help build the modern nation. The attention to symbolic work produced the first modern form of state propaganda. The revolutionaries also learned from the monarchy's prior investment in spectacle that for change to take hold among the people, it needed to be founded on words and abstract principles as well as visual representation. New rituals produced a new way of life.

The Old Regime's power establishment, which included king and nobility, topped the list of the revolutionaries' targets, who knew their legitimacy had been grounded in the traditional power of the Catholic Church. The revolution thus confronted that institution head on. They seized church lands; priests were forced to swear an allegiance to the Revolution so they would not be in the employ of a foreign power (the pope). Revolutionaries closed churches, beheaded the sculptures of kings that adorned cathedrals; melted church bells and church treasures. In 1791, the government transformed the newly built church to the patron saint of Paris, Saint Geneviève, into a pantheon where the great men of the Revolution and the nation would be collectively memorialized. Old symbols were discarded and new ones fabricated.

The attack on the Roman Catholic Church also ushered in attempts to create a civic religion inspired by the writings of Jean-Jacques Rousseau. The revolutionaries organized a series of festivals, the first major "stadium" events since antiquity. There, among enormous crowds, French people enacted belonging to the new social order while lighting bonfires and burning crowns. They planted liberty trees and sang songs declaring adherence to the principles of liberty, equality, and fraternity. More explicitly, in November 1793, the goddess of Liberty, played by an actress, presided over a "Festival of Reason" within the walls of the Cathedral of Notre Dame.

The new government also usurped the Catholic Church's control of the fundamental life cycle rituals: birth, marriage, and death—all of which would now be registered at the city hall rather than at the local church. Civil marriage remains obligatory in France up to this day. Newly conceived as a civil contract, marriage could also be undone. The Revolution thus instated the most radical divorce law on the Continent in 1792 because it could be decreed by mutual consent and was available to all social classes. But under the Napoleonic Code of 1804, rights regressed as it became impossible for women to initiate a divorce. When the monarchy returned, so did the prohibition on divorce (as of 1816). Civil divorce was not permanently reinstituted in France until 1884.

The Republic protected its citizens against priests and established direct relations between male citizens as equals and between individual male citizens and their state. The disestablishment of religion enfranchised religious minorities, notably Protestants and Jews. As Count Stanislas Marie Adélaide de Clermont-Tonnerre explained in 1789, "We must refuse everything to the Jews as a nation and accord everything to the Jews as individuals." The state would extend individual liberty but insisted on the renunciation of any competing group identity. This notion has evolved over time into the Republican concept of "laïcité," which can be thought of as state secularism. Although France officially separated church and state only in 1905, a battle had raged since the Revolution about what role, if any, the church could have in the ever-expanding horizon of government schools founded as part of the modern state. Since then, secularism has generally denoted keeping public life free of religion, which the state considers an entirely personal matter. It is impossible, however, given the remarkable anticlericalism of the Revolution and of the Republicanism it established, not to understand that there is a sense that the state is free *from* religion rather than there to preserve religious freedoms in France.

Fraternity, here again, functions as the key term. Religious differences among citizens who are guaranteed equality under the law and the freedom to worship could nevertheless be perceived as barriers to bonds among equals. This original interpretation of "fraternité" has been perpetuated by the modern French state's official indifference to religious, ethnic, and racial difference. It is this same absolute privileging of universal and natural individual human rights that would later be used, first by the Army of the Republic and then by French forces during periods of imperial expansion, to impose the values of the Revolution on militarily defeated peoples in the name of equality. If fraternity is taken to its logical extreme it makes perfect sense that the emerging nation-state would also be imperial in its formation.

If the Revolution was made in words and images, and accordingly spread globally, it was spoken in French. One of the great beneficiaries of the Revolution was the French language itself. The already widespread influence of the French language on educated people across Europe and North America on the eve of the Revolution contributed to the strength of the Revolution itself. At the same time, the Revolution also helped standardize French among the French population. Since the first article of the initial Constitution of the Republic defined free public education as its principal social goal, education became fundamental to the revolutionary agenda. Early language surveys showed that among the 27 to 28 million people one could count as French, only 3 million fluently spoke Parisian French, which defined the standard, perhaps ironically, as the "king's French." Having dispensed with the clergy who had previously provided whatever little schooling was available, the Convention voted to establish a system of free and compulsory education for boys and girls—the first such system anywhere. The Convention worked to eradicate the linguistic corruptions of local languages. Because the Assembly had earlier rearranged France into eighty-three relatively uniform departments (or districts), such national projects became easier to imagine, if difficult to complete, since the state did not yet have an ample supply of educators to promulgate the new symbolic culture of 1789 and beyond.

Making the nation over time and in place

The revolutionaries sought to remake time by introducing a new calendar that began at the end of the monarchy and thus inaugurated a new era of historical sensibility. History and historical thinking emerged from the period of the Revolution; the idea of nostalgia, the interest in ruins and memoirs are testament to this new form of consciousness. For France, the Revolution also launched a great social project of education about the newly constituted nation, and the nineteenth century produced a rich and dedicated literature about French history as part of the foundation of Republican society. The textbook author Ernest Lavisse, born a generation after the first Revolution, reflected in his memoirs on the impact of the Revolutionary tradition: "We believed that the Republic would liberate not only France but all humanity, which awaited our signal." To this end, he first wrote a general "universal history" that explained France's important place in the world and then dedicated himself to following in the footsteps of the great historian of an earlier generation, Jules Michelet, by setting out to write the history of his own nation.

Lavisse is best known for his primary school textbook, written in 1884 and revised many times. In such basic texts one can understand the way history became the basis for the formation of national mythology. The book's cover, addressed directly to the children who would read it, counseled: "You should love France because nature made her beautiful and history made her great." In this comment we also see what amounts to a geographic obsession that may be a fundamental part of most nineteenth-century nationalist rhetoric, but whose specificity in France has helped shape its modern history. After all, France is not a natural geographic expression such as an island or peninsula. It has in the twentieth century finally come to be called the Hexagon, perhaps only as a defensive move against its dwindling empire.

The Revolution was so concerned with matters of the physical contours of the French state that it reorganized them internally, doing away with the divisions of the provinces that had been handed down mostly as feudal duchies and baronies integrated by the already centralizing powers of the monarchy. France had a good head start in this process because, starting in the 1740s, it was the first European country to make comprehensive national maps. Erasing the historical identities associated with the old system, the departments (eighty-three in 1789, now expanded to ninety-six with an additional four overseas departments) were named after significant natural and geographic features, mostly rivers (the Seine and the Garonne, for example) and mountains

(Alps, Pyrenees). This may have worked to naturalize these new artificial state-created divisions, but it also embedded a department's identity in the land.

Nineteenth-century French geographers produced a narrative that conceived of France as a crossroads of Europe. The geographer Paul Vidal de la Blache noted that France was a space "in which the lines delineating the larger continental mass come together and almost converge in such a way as to trace a sort of bridge between the Mediterranean and the Atlantic." Of course, it also attached to the Continent to the east and the south. For Vidal this bridge offered France an advantage, since he also believed that "no civilized country is the exclusive artisan of its own civilization." The geographic situation of France has proven to be decisive over time, for example, in such instances as the two world wars. In World War I, the trenches ran down France on the western side of the Western Front; thus many of the French soldiers, who died in proportionately higher numbers than any of the other major combatants, died on their own soil. During World War II, France did not have England's geographic advantage of being an island, however much Hitler attempted to transcend the limits of the land and sea with aerial bombardments. The obsessive planning that went into the defensive fortifications, known as the Maginot Line, which were built along the French borders with Germany during the period between the world wars, dug that idea of France right into the ground. As a result, the place of France also continues to play a role in international war commemorations. Approximately 4,400 non-French Allied troops and an estimated 5,000–9,000 German forces lost their lives in the D-Day battles of World War II and are laid to rest in cemeteries there. Victors and vanquished still meet on French ground when they seek to remember both world wars.

Physically, France offered a remarkably diverse set of natural conditions in a relatively compact space. Out of this diversity and the exchange between neighbors and regions—and the more contact a region had with other regions and even other nations, the more vital it was thought to be—a unity formed. France was, in Vidal's words again: "a land seemingly made to absorb the greatest part of its own emigration." The importance of geography also attests to one of the realities of France—it remained a primarily rural society until 1933 when, for the first time, the number of city-dwellers out-paced rural populations. In 1800, one-third of the population still lived in self-governing village-states of thirty-five inhabitants or fewer.

Despite these internal migrations and de-ruralization, agricultural production has remained an important part of French life. France is currently the European Union's largest agricultural producer and the world's second-largest agricultural exporter, behind the United States. Wherever the French population actually lives, the sentiments expressed by Vidal certainly took root in the collective mentality of the French in the nineteenth century. He wrote, "What the Frenchman sees in France... is the bounty of the earth and the pleasure of living on it."

In the nineteenth century, writers and citizens "discovered" and defined France as an entity as geographic mythology took hold. By almost all measures, localism could be consonant with the broader centralization project of the state, and the very richness in its diversity became one of modern France's great boasts: its more than 300 cheeses, 250 wines, natural wonders such as the Alps (first scaled in the nineteenth century), and remarkable traces of the ancient past such as the first-century bridge, the Pont du Gard, attested to the fact that modern France was also ancient Gaul (and its boundaries are more or less the same). The Tour de France bicycle race embodies and exploits the nation's rich geographic diversity. Even before the establishment of the race, *Le Tour de France par deux enfants*, a popular school primer, first published in 1877, was used to teach French history and geography, and taught this lesson of unity in diversity. The tale recounts the adventures of two young boys from the eastern provinces of France that had recently been lost to Germany in the Franco-Prussian War. Julien and André journey across their country in order to instill in French children lessons (complete with more than two hundred illustrations) about how regional diversity is one of France's great national strengths.

Despite the emphasis on geographic accounts of rural life, it was cities, and Paris in particular, that eventually made order out of the diversity and moved the nation forward. For Jules Michelet, Paris functioned to organize the local into the central. "The center knows itself and knows all the rest," he offered, explaining that local particularisms could only be tolerated if they were eventually subordinated in favor of the nation's center in Paris, traditional home of its monarchs and seat of its modern national government.

If writers celebrated local diversity, the French state's powers of centralization over the course of the nineteenth century did perhaps turn peasants into Frenchmen, a well-worn epithet about state modernization in France. In particular, the Republican schools taught the national language, and such books as those by Vidal and Lavisse also conveyed urban dwellers' values to the countryside. New roads and the railways especially enhanced communication and brought the French into greater contact with each other and with Paris (where, like Rome, all roads figuratively and literally led). The army forged a group out of the male population who fought in the name of the whole—a nationalist sentiment that could then be brought back to the villages when the soldiers returned from military duty.

The history complex

Despite the prominence of geography in constructing an image of the nation, it ultimately took a back seat to history as the central means of national mythologizing since the Revolution. History in modern France became overtly political (and still is) as the Revolution helped foster a new historical consciousness. Having

participated in spectacular historical celebrations such as the
Festival of the Federation a year after the fall of the Bastille in
1790, and having watched the guillotine busily at work in the
Place de la Révolution, citizens knew that history happened by
human action. Ernest Renan, one of the most articulate theorists
of the nation in the nineteenth century, insisted in his "What is a
Nation?" lecture of 1882 that neither race, nor language, nor
religion, nor geography made a nation. Aside from the will to
share a common destiny, he explained that a common past defined
the nation. "A heroic past, great men, glory...this is the spiritual
capital on which the idea of the nation rests."

The French Revolution may have catapulted France into the
future, but it also generated a preoccupation with writing about
the French past. The period after the Revolution produced a
stylistic vogue for not only Greek and Roman antiquity but also
for the Middle Ages (including the mid-nineteenth century
restorations of medieval cathedrals). In addition, historical fiction,
such as Victor Hugo's *Notre Dame de Paris* and *Ninety-Three*,
Honoré de Balzac's *Les Chouans*, and Alexandre Dumas's more
popular novels *The Three Musketeers* and *Queen Margot*,
flourished, enlivening the past for French readers.

But the history obsession also produced two of the perhaps most
overproduced of national heroes: Napoleon and Joan of Arc. They
inspired plays, novels, sculptures, paintings, songs, and mounds of
kitsch in trinkets. Napoleon's life, one could argue, is the stuff of
which legend is made. His military career took flight after his
successful tactics led him to defend the Revolutionary forces in
the siege of Toulon in 1793; thereafter he was put in charge of the
French army in Italy. His career continued to rise when he
narrowly missed being executed as a Robespierrist in 1794. With
the proverbial "whiff of grapeshot" in 1795, once again used to
counter rebellion against the Revolution in Paris, the young son of
a Corsican noble, emerged as the commander of the Army of the
Interior. Within four years, Napoleon would rule France; he soon

put Europe on a tumultuous path of continuous warfare for fifteen years, while ruling the largest empire in Europe since antiquity.

Napoleon began fabricating his own glory during his lifetime with the strong censorship of all theater, books, and art, a massive program of "Empire style" complete with images of the emperor, and his twin symbols, the imperial eagle and the bee (associated with Childeric, father of Clovis, and thus the oldest symbol of the French monarchy). The great Revolutionary artist Jacques-Louis David served as his court painter, but Napoleon also enlisted others such as Antoine-Jean Gros and Jean-Auguste-Dominique Ingres to put a glittery patina on his rule. His death in exile on St. Helena after the defeat at Waterloo and its mysterious circumstances only helped fuel the attachment to the former emperor. In 1821, the year of his death, more than 108 books were published about him and his empire in France. During 1830–31, more than twenty-five plays about him opened in Parisian theaters.

Few careers have as spectacular a fifteen-year period as Napoleon's between 1799 and 1814, and whether he is seen as son of the Revolution or its betrayer, one cannot dispute that the physically small man was historically grand. Thus the Napoleon industry after his death is in some measure a continuation of the legacy he began to perpetuate while he was alive. In 1833 his statue was restored to the top of the Vendôme column; in 1840 his body, which had been buried on the island of his exile in the South Atlantic, was returned to France. It took twenty years to prepare the tomb in which he rests at the Invalides, the military hospital turned pantheon. Hitler made sure to visit there when he made his tour of Paris not long after it fell to the Germans in 1940. When the emperor's nephew Louis-Napoleon exploited the legend to make himself "emperor of the French" during the mid-nineteenth century, the government became the prime mover in the Napoleon industry that continues to this day. The complexity and contradictions in Napoleon and his legacy perhaps make him the perfect hero for the French—a people that have made a habit of accepting that nothing is entirely black or white when it comes to political life.

Joan of Arc would seem, at first sight, to be less modern than Napoleon, but her major nineteenth-century comeback is a true Napoleonic effect. She shares with the emperor the status of unlikely heroine. A peasant girl, she changed the course of history by driving the English out of France during the last stages of the Hundred Years War in 1429. She was eventually captured in battle, sold to the English, tried by the Inquisition, and burned at the stake for heresy. In the nineteenth century, Catholic forces of anti-Republicanism, seeking to remind the French how important a vision-inspired peasant had been to the kingdom, sought to have her canonized as a saint, which happened in 1920. Republicans knew she was a democrat and woman of the people who died a martyr, betrayed by the institutions of the Old Regime they hated: the monarchy and the Catholic Church. Known as the "sainte de la patrie," she offered a vision of a patron saint of an invaded nation (not unlike Saint Geneviève, the patron saint of Paris whose prayers were said to have spared the city from a visit by Attila the Hun, who went to Orléans instead). Michelet dedicated 130 pages to her in his fifth volume of the *History of France* (1844) in which this daughter of the poor incarnates the people of France and unites them as a nation: "She loved France so much! ... And France, touched, began to love herself."

If during the nineteenth century, Republicans and their opponents alike could embrace Joan, she has since become a cult figure of the political Right, especially championed by virulent nationalist anti-Semites and the Vichy regime, who associated her with a Frenchness that was rooted in the soil and who also saw themselves as betrayed by the British. But there is something in her story about the miracle that saved France in its darkest hour that still appeals to a nation simultaneously aware and cynical enough to see both the real social problems of the moment and act to change them while remaining idealistic enough to believe that destiny has preordained them to survive and play a role in world affairs. It is not really that far from Joan of Arc to General Charles de Gaulle, who led the French government twice during and after World War II.

The French political tradition since the revolution

French politics since the Revolution has steered a course between rupture and tradition, action and destiny. In the opening pages of Charles de Gaulle's memoir, he explained that France had a special role to play: "providence has created her for complete successes or for exemplary misfortunes." De Gaulle, general of the Free French forces during World War II and the most influential leader in France since Napoleon never to wear a crown, looked back at the revolutionary tradition with a great deal of skepticism and concern. For him, French history stretched back to the conversion of the Merovingian King Clovis (471–511) to Christianity and reached a sort of apex under Louis XIV. The Revolution had brought factionalism and disunity by virtue of the breaking of the social bonds of the feudal order. And, looking back at France after the defeat in 1940, it may be more than reasonable to have had less faith in the Republican tradition than in the heady days of the short-lived Popular Front in the mid-1930s, which had guaranteed workers their first paid vacations and empowered French unions as never before.

Political instability characterized much of French history from the Revolution to World War II with a sense that the battle for the Republic and what it meant was always being replayed. In the more than two hundred years since 1789, only the Third Republic (1870–1940) and now the Fifth (1958–) lasted well over a decade. The Revolution ushered in a period of political experimentation rather than political stability with its five Republics, two monarchies, two empires, and one proto-fascist "French State."

Although the Republic created a new democratic political culture, it continued the long tradition of warfare that had helped consolidate the monarchy in the early-modern period. Through the political turmoil of the French state since 1789, all governments advocated for their vision in the language of the Revolution; even during Vichy, France's most conservative incarnation, the geriatric Marshall Pétain called for a National Revolution. Not only were the French the first to proclaim the universal "rights of man," which the United Nations made the standard of international justice in 1948; in 1848, in another upheaval that would produce the Second Republic (1848–51) after the period of monarchical restoration following Napoleon, France was the first country to institute universal male suffrage. While Napoleon may have been the zenith of French military power, French colonial expansion also continued throughout the nineteenth and into the twentieth century, subjugating other people in the name of their eventual promised liberty.

Conflict in France since the Revolution has also included more than its fair share of internal strife in the form of what the French call "guerres franco-françaises," or civil wars. Perhaps few episodes in the history of such internal conflict are as dramatic as the Paris Commune of 1870–71, which pitted the government of National Defense, which replaced the defeated Emperor Napoleon III, against the Parisian-elected government that pronounced itself "The Commune." This radical and short-lived government, which Marx thought would provide the model for the dictatorship of the proletariat, returned to the Revolutionary calendar, declared a separation between church and state, gave pensions to unmarried companions of men who had died in the Franco-Prussian war, and declared a moratorium on back rent owed, along with other radical social changes enacted in its two months in power. In a confrontation that produced the bloodiest week in French history, the government, headquartered at Versailles, executed between 25,000 and 30,000 Parisians while Communards burned important centers of government authority: the police headquarters, city hall, and the Tuileries Palace, which had managed to survive the prior insurrections in the streets of Paris. The Commune also produced some of the earliest highly politicized uses of photographs, among them Eugène Appert's work depicting the "bloody week." These works sutured real and staged moments to bolster the view of the savagery of the crimes of the Commune. For example, in one photo, distributed in the small "carte de visite" format, the photographer reenacted an execution and cut in photos of the Commune's seemingly innocent victims, many of them priests. Whether used as propaganda to bolster the government's suppression of the Communards after the fact or as evidence of the early acceptance of composite photography as a form of photojournalism, the Commune also updated and modernized the visual program of the revolutionary tradition.

2. The victims, bystanders, and firing squad are each pasted in to this photomontage of the "Assassination of the Hostages in the Prison of La Roquette" in Eugène Appert's series "The Crimes of the Commune."

What happened in France did not stay in France. As Metternich is supposed to have said not long after the Congress of Vienna, "When France sneezes, Europe catches cold." Responses to change in France included the many British denunciations of the first Revolution, the European-wide movement known as Romanticism, which at once reflected the nationalism of the Revolutionary era but also lionized the individual. In 1848, especially, the founding of the Second French Republic in the wake of the collapse of the July Monarchy (1830–48) offered inspiration to other liberal revolutions in the Austrian Empire, Germany, and Italy. Perhaps most influentially, Karl Marx endowed France with great importance, as he studied those revolutions with care while living in France. Later radicals steeped in Marxism, from Lenin to Mao to Ho Chi Minh, made it their business to study the course of French political life in the century after the Revolution because they understood it as a model for the future of world politics. As Lenin wrote, "The road to Paris lies through Peking."

When the Republic stabilized by 1877, external relations figured strongly in the course of French Republican politics. Colonial expansion and military conquest continued up until World War II as part of the Republican agenda. Despite strong leftist pacifism, the entire political spectrum in France came together as the Republic entered World War I in 1914 after Germany declared war on France's Russian ally. For many participants and historians ever since, that war opened a new culture of barbarism and technologically wrought destruction. Four long years of war ended in a pyrrhic victory for France marked by population devastation and an unwieldy peace with Germany. This eventually led to the most humiliating moment in modern French history: the defeat of June 1940 and the subsequent occupation by Germany during the course of the war. French collaboration became the policy of the Vichy government that replaced "Liberty, Equality, and Fraternity" with another tripartite slogan: "Work, Family and Fatherland." Despite its embrace of revolutionary rhetoric, Vichy abandoned

the "rights of man" especially for Jews. The problem of the
Republic's values beyond French borders, and the application of
those values to the immigrants within them, have since produced
some of the deepest contradictions and complications in modern
French history.

Leading the nation

Charles de Gaulle had a "certain idea of France," as he wrote in his
1954 war memoirs. That idea was that "France could not be
France without grandeur." In his personal style and through his
actions, he sought to follow one fundamental aspect of Napoleonic
rule: he believed that the leader embodied the nation. He
preferred to speak directly to the citizenry, often using the new
medium of television in an especially canny manner.

Both during and after the war, de Gaulle made leadership one of
his vital issues. On the one hand, he sought to restore France's
autonomy as a nation but understood its future as part of
something fundamentally European and supported those postwar
developments that resulted in the European Union. He also
oversaw the dismantling of the French Empire, especially
withdrawing from Algeria in a bloody conflict (1954–62) in which
he had to protect his own life from the French army officers who
struggled to keep Algeria French. Having come to power at the
Liberation, de Gaulle left the government with the adoption of the
constitution of the Fourth Republic (1946–58), which he
considered insufficiently strong since it favored the legislature
over the president. When problems in Algeria led to a near
collapse of that Republic, the government returned to de Gaulle,
who interrupted the writing of his memoirs to lead again. His
terms included six months of emergency control and the
opportunity to write a new constitution. In that constitution, the
presidency became much more powerful than before, although it
was not until 1962 that the constitution was amended to have the
people directly elect the president.

The strong presidency included a seven-year term (reduced to five years in 2000 in order to avoid what became known as "cohabitation"—a system in which the president and the prime minister, who represents the Assembly, are from different parties). In the years since de Gaulle, the Socialist François Mitterrand served two terms and thus governed the longest among Fifth Republic presidents. Despite many economic nationalization efforts that ended in failure, he left a classically "imperial" trace of his presidency by rebuilding Paris in the tradition of the two Napoleons through his "Grands Travaux" project, which bestowed upon Paris a new opera house, a new national library, a renovated Louvre, and even a new triumphal arch at the business park at city's western edge known as La Défense.

The twenty-first century has produced Nicolas Sarkozy, a president who is as flamboyant as any has been so far. The son of a Hungarian immigrant and a mother of Franco-Catholic-Sephardic Jewish heritage, Sarkozy was elected as a conservative and yet remains attached to such revolutionary concepts as "the people" and "change." Upon his election, he declared the French people the winner as they had "not given up the battle" nor had they chosen to remain trapped in "immobility and conservatism." Perhaps respected more outside France than in his own country, Sarkozy has been controversial. He called young rioters in the suburbs "scum" (*racaille*); he established the French Council for Muslim Cults in order to do what France did with the Jews in the nineteenth century: pointedly call for assimilation in order to assure that they become French first and foremost. He appointed the first woman of non-European descent, Rachida Dati, to a position in his cabinet.

Perhaps most unusual and even troubling to some in France is that he is not a product of an elite military or intellectual education. Since the Fifth Republic, French leaders on both the Right and the Left have sat in the same classrooms at the *grandes écoles*, especially the Ecole Nationale de l'Administration. This rule by a homogenously educated elite has been replaced in Sarkozy's government by lawyers and business people much more in keeping with what can perhaps be identified as an Americanization of French public life. He believes the French people themselves are far closer to embracing American-style food, shopping, and work habits than the elite political class that surely has more to lose with change. Sarkozy even jogs.

What Sarkozy also represents is the arrival of a leader who is not building politics on the shoulders of the giants of modern French political history. It may be less of a deliberate plan than a tactic resulting from ignorance and perhaps even a healthy lack of appreciation for the French past. The struggle over the meaning of France continues, but as the Republic is now firmly entrenched and also embedded within the greater European Union, the political organization of the state has taken a back seat to concerns over nationality in the postcolonial, multiethnic society that France has become. Of the once-useful myths of history and geography that helped establish France as modern, the French Revolution as a singular event consisting of rapid and radical actions, bolstered by rich and meaningful symbolism, continues to energize France not simply because it keeps change embedded into the fabric of French political life but also because it defines a mission in which France acts in the name of the good of humanity. That vision keeps the Revolution both foundational and incomplete. This is the sort of past that will always have a future.

Chapter 2
French and the civilizing mission

All nations claim a special mission. For France, that mission has been culture. The nation's role on a global scale since 1789 is complex but has rested on a commitment to cultural dissemination rather than mere military and administrative imperial conquest. The French state, first the monarchy and then the Republic, developed a sense of its relative importance vis-à-vis other powers, based on the idea that cultural influence really matters and that attraction and seduction rather than coercion are vital qualities in establishing international influence. For France, culture had to be disseminated. France has regarded itself as having a "civilizing mission," which included being charged with propagating the idea of a world cultural heritage while putting things French at its apex.

The Revolution inherited many ideals from the Old Regime it overthrew. The nature of the cultural project and its importance has a long history in which France cast itself as the inheritor of the greatness of Rome. From the time of France's Renaissance king, Francis I, the court tied itself to that classical achievement and, in fact, imported many antiquities from Italy. It also imported artists, such as Leonardo da Vinci, into its network of patronage. This is how the *Mona Lisa* came to reside in France. During the reign of Louis XIV, the French court became the height of classical taste. The king created the French art academy in Rome and had copies of many of the great sculptures made and brought to his court in Versailles, which then became the best single place to contemplate the heritage of antiquity. This project would later be extended in the establishment of the Louvre as a public museum in 1793. If the French state saw itself as bearing the mantle of Western civilization generally construed, it also promoted the notion that its language would come to explain and transmit that heritage around the world. To disseminate such a heritage, the world would need to learn perfect French.

The French obsession with the value and meaning of the written word has served as the basis by which France disseminated its culture, an especially canny strategy in a world of increasing literacy. Since the Enlightenment, many proponents of France suggested that the French language had an innate clarity and rationality that made learning it an ideal unto itself. On the eve of the Revolution, European aristocrats, even as far away as Russia, were already linguistically under the spell of France. By the eighteenth century, Russian aristocrats learned French from birth, taught by their governesses, while they learned Russian from the servants. Frederick the Great of Prussia was said to speak German like a coachman (to his horse) but French with his family and social equals.

French culture has been as embodied in language and the dissemination of the written word as it has been in political ideas or material objects. The durability of France is based upon its fixation on language, its focus on the importance of writers and intellectuals, and the development of institutions associated with the power of the word. These elements, joined with a notion that French culture was, in fact, universal, made France not just an imperial power in formal terms but enabled and continues to enable France to play a role in the world that extends far beyond the borders of the nation and its former empire.

French lessons

The writer Albert Camus declared, "My homeland is the French language." These words, by a writer born to French parents living in Algeria, suggest that *Francophonie* constituted its own universe. Camus's status as a Frenchman in Algeria also underscores the imperial aspects of such a notion. French is the only language other than English to be taught in every country where there is foreign language instruction, and it trails only English as the second language of choice at the dawn of the twenty-first century. French is one of four languages (English, Spanish, and Arabic are the others) that has official status in more than twenty countries. It is fair to claim that French is still the "other" global language after English.

Language as a touchstone of cultural life predates the modern period. When François I issued the Ordinance of Villers-Cotterêts in 1539 that concerned the powers of the French state against the papacy, he also struck a policy in which all official documents would be produced in French, rather than Latin. The Renaissance king may have been deeply influenced by Italian culture, but his policy was designed to promote the use of French and thus his kingdom. The fact that he ruled early in the history of the explosion of publishing made possible by the invention of the printing press also contributed to the vast number of works written and circulated in French. His reign also coincided with the rise of Protestantism, which favored the use of the vernacular French, since Latin was the language of the Roman Catholic Church.

By the time of the Enlightenment, French had become the language of diplomacy as well as the lingua franca of court societies throughout Europe. The spread of the French language was aided by the odd notion, especially for a living vernacular, that it had a pure form. French seemed to have an authentic source in the region of Paris. The creation of the French Academy in 1635 by the Cardinal de Richelieu institutionalized this idea. Like many Old Regime French innovations, the cardinal modeled his institute after an Italian one: the Accademia della Crusca in Florence. In particular, the new academy made French the first European language to have an official dictionary and a fully developed system of spelling and grammar, for which forty appointed "immortals" are still charged with updating. Such codification made it much easier for non-native French speakers to learn the language. The Académie française served as the first but certainly not the last institution that has maintained a close tie between France and French, despite the global spread of the language ever since.

In 1782 the Berlin Academy asked, "How has French become the world's universal language?" suggesting what a given the ubiquity of French had become on the eve of the Revolution. As France became an increasingly powerful and wealthy nation, the French language also became associated with those qualities. Within France, the development of the salons, social gatherings outside of the court, which prized the clever use of language above all, contributed to the association of linguistic skill with social status. Aristocrats and social climbers throughout Europe imitated this form of sociability, including speaking in French. The salons were tied to the Enlightenment movement through wealthy female patrons who provided the new thinkers known as the *philosophes* with financial support. Notably, the great publication project of the late eighteenth century, the *Encyclopédie*, received financial backing from the king's mistress, Madame de Pompadour, and the Russian empress, Catherine II, the latter of whom sustained the project by buying the library of its editor, Denis Diderot, which she allowed him to keep until the end of his life. The singularity of the twenty-eight-volume work alone helped associate French with the most novel and systematic thought in the world. At the time, because literacy was relatively limited and because few projects reached that scale, a single language could appear to monopolize the great written works. That such a storehouse of seemingly universal knowledge was written in French helped associate France with a vision of universal rather than the particular culture, as is often the case with powerful nations and their cultures.

Civilization and empire

The idea of civilization itself developed in the eighteenth century because intellectuals sought a way to define the triumph of ideas such as reason. Civilization as a unitary concept came to mean the opposite of barbarism, which had once simply been used to define non-Christians. On the eve of the Revolution, the French more or less already believed the rest of the world needed civilizing and that they had the universal culture ready-made for such work.

The Revolution helped tie the civilizing mission to language. Within France the revolutionaries sought to eradicate local languages such as Breton; the French military campaigns of the revolutionary and Napoleonic eras "freed" people to think and learn in French. As the French Empire expanded, especially in the late nineteenth and early twentieth centuries, the notion of the civilizing mission became part and parcel of French imperial expansion. Inspired by the Revolution's universalizing principles, the civilizing mission surely became a tool of imperial expansion.

The system of French imperial expansion dates back to the sixteenth-century French explorations in Canada and mid-seventeenth-century colonization and commerce in Martinique, Senegal, and India. As a system that is inherently unequal and whose existence was maintained by the idea of the French civilizing mission, it came under scrutiny during the French Revolution. The Declaration of the Rights of Man and Citizen of 1789 forbade slavery in France but did not extend this liberation to the colonies until slavery was abolished everywhere by the Convention in 1794 for pragmatic and ideological reasons. French law was extended to French colonies in 1795 as part of liberating peoples from Old Regime tyrannies and inequality everywhere.

With a sense of both right and duty, the French nation continued to expand outward throughout Europe and the wider world. The French conquered Algeria, the first Arab territory annexed by the West (1830), islands in the Pacific (especially New Caledonia, 1853), Senegal (1854–65), the short-lived Mexican misadventure (1861–67), Cochinchina (Vietnam, 1862), and Cambodia (1863). The French Third Republic managed the last major French colonial expansion into the Maghreb (Morocco and Tunisia were added), Syria, and Lebanon as well as French West and French East Africa, Laos, Madagascar, Togo, and Cameroon. By the end of World War I, the French Empire spanned 11 million kilometers and had 100 million inhabitants, about twice the size of the population of metropolitan France.

If all European countries colonized in the name of their cultural superiority, the French not only colonized in their language but also in its name. Colonial policy may have changed over the course of the development of the French empire, but one issue was never in doubt: the French language would be taught and learned—not simply to ease communication between colonizer and colonized but because it was a cornerstone in the development of civilization. After all, if all the courts of Europe were already speaking French, how could it not be central in the transformation and improvement of the peoples they encountered in the colonial arena?

The value of the French language was bolstered in the nineteenth century by the creation of a national education system, first under the historian and statesman François Guizot in the mid-century and then under Prime Minister Jules Ferry, who helped lead the Third Republic in creating mandatory and secular public education. Since France still had enormous linguistic diversity, one of the primary goals of the new French schools was to teach all French people residing in France to speak "proper" French. Through the course of the century the focus on the instruction of French produced books of grammar (*Le Bescherelle*, as the handbook named after its author came to be known) and methods for teaching the language, perhaps the best known of which were designed by Pierre Larousse, who also authored a major dictionary.

As the French bureaucracy and the state itself expanded, the Académie provided the standard French on which the new government exams would be based. This created an idealized form of French: no matter how many native Francophones there were outside France in such places as Canada and Louisiana, the notion of a pure and true French, disseminated from France, remains to this day. The notion of an ideal French also helps explain the obsession with dictation, meant to weed out imperfections and faults in the written language. It is also why we can still dispute whether using the feminine for a female teacher or minister (Madame/la professeur; Madame/le ministre) is correct. In French, *professeur* is a masculine noun, irrespective of the individual who occupies the post. (The government now endorses gender consistency as in "Madame, la professeur," but the French Academy does not.)

Educational policy and the teaching of French also formed a cornerstone of successful imperial expansion. Jules Ferry, who had a hand in empire as well as education, believed French expansion was meant to spread French language, customs, and genius. Yet one of the great ironies of French colonial education rested on the fact that the Roman Catholic Church, the object of the Republic's greatest scorn, was charged with a great deal of the transmission of its values in the colonial arena. Bilingual missionaries were among the most effective teachers of French in the colonies. In some places, such as Lebanon, the French took responsibility for the Christian community, whose presence dated back to the Crusades in the twelfth century. In the nineteenth century, the

French negotiated with the Ottoman Empire to establish a special protected territory on Mount Lebanon for the Maronite Christians. After World War I and the defeat of the Ottoman Empire, France was given the geographic area covering Syria and Lebanon because of the already successful linguistic colonization. In Algeria, where a European population of mixed nationality of French, Italians, and Portuguese, along with a relatively sizable Jewish population formed approximately 1.5 million of a population of 4 million, French succeeded in becoming part of the linguistic landscape. Although only 25 percent of the Arabic-speaking population attended the French school system that developed there over the course of the nineteenth century, the indigenous population learned French in part because of work and in part because, as a department of France, French served as the language of administration.

Beyond empire

The linguistic and cultural influence of France, its "rayonnement," (influence or radiance) has far exceeded any specifically imperial project. French terms pervade in many languages from the use of the term "cinema" to "denim" (from "De Nîmes," the place where the blue cloth originally was made). In short, the French legacy of cultural influence is as significant as its formal imperial influence. On the eve of World War I, French was the most spoken Western language in the Middle East, having replaced Italian and Greek after 1860. The building of the Suez Canal by a French company, opened in 1869, also helped develop French influence in the region. In Romania, where the inhabitants already spoke a Romance language, educated people also started to learn French, and it became the language with which they spoke to Russians and Greek administrators of the Ottoman Empire.

French influence extended to many places far outside the boundaries of the French Empire. For example, Simón Bolívar, the democratic liberator of much of Latin America, turned to France for inspiration. Buenos Aires even became known as "Little Paris." In these cases and unlike in the colonies, locally powerful families introduced French culture and associated it with legitimating their own local superiority and rule over "uncultured" and primitive indigenous populations. As had been the case in the eighteenth century, French became the second language of countries such as Argentina, and many French teachers moved there to help with this effort of language instruction. In classrooms in Buenos Aires, students absorbed lessons that instructed them that "Paris is the capital of the civilized world," and they were encouraged to visit. Beyond Algeria, which technically was part of France, more French nationals lived in Argentina than anywhere outside France. Despite French cultural influence, the British remained the economic powerhouse of informal empire in Argentina. What this suggests is that influence and power come in many forms, and for the French, culture and language have always played a predominant role.

The French education system also spread far beyond the colonies with the implantation of French junior high and high schools that follow a French curriculum and usually employ French nationals to teach in them. In the Ottoman Empire, more than five hundred French schools enrolled approximately 100,000 students by the turn of the twentieth century. Hoping to spread the French language as a universal glue, private individuals created the *Alliance française* in 1883. The system, which now consists of more than one thousand branches operating in 136 countries, was modeled on a mid-nineteenth-century Paris-based Jewish project, the *Alliance Israélite Universelle*, which sought to uplift (and Europeanize) the world's Jewish populations through education and acculturation in French. The Alliance française also published books for teaching French as a foreign language. In the 1953 introduction to one such book, readers were informed that "French uplifts and serves." By virtue of the success of the *Alliance française* system, the Ministry of Foreign Affairs added the position of cultural attaché to its foreign postings, the first among major powers to envision a position dedicated to spreading a national culture in foreign locations.

The French government developed a robust set of institutions of cultural diplomacy, among them the *Association Française d'action artistique*, *Unifrance Films*, and finally the Ministry of Culture in 1958. President de Gaulle selected the writer André Malraux to head this newfangled organization. De Gaulle was opposed by the leftist intellectuals of the day such as Jean-Paul Sartre, but he craved the participation of a writer and intellectual in his government. The Ministry of Culture had as its mission, according to its own foundational literature, "to make humanity's greatest masterpieces, and especially those of France, accessible to the greatest possible number of French people; to reach the largest possible audience with our cultural heritage, and to promote the creation of works of art and of the intellect which will further enrich it." Malraux's ministry directed theater, the Opéra, the cinema, and French museums, and was responsible for literary promotion. His ministry created "Houses of Culture" throughout France to assure the continued internal cultural colonization of their own country. When de Gaulle said, according to Malraux, that "Every man who writes...and writes well, serves France," he was not only explaining why he might have appointed a writer such as Malraux to revitalize French culture under the government's supervision. He laid bare another truism about France: a long-established respect for writers and intellectuals.

Writers and intellectuals

Writers enjoy a special status in France. If under the Old Regime, literature became part of the eminence of the king's brilliance, words also became central to imagining the world in opposition to the king. Writers such as Jean-Jacques Rousseau were read with great ardor as revolutionary creed, but the Revolution also made clear that writers could use the pen as others had used the sword. Jean-Paul Marat, the revolutionary journalist whose legacy lives on in David's remarkable painting of his murder by Charlotte Corday (*Death of Marat*), was assassinated in response to the poison of his pen. Much of the great literature of the nineteenth century for which France is well known was also part of political and social engagement, and was understood as both powerful and dangerous. During authoritarian regimes, social critics such as the Romantic writer Madame de Staël fled and sought exile because she had criticized Napoleon as a tyrant in her writings. The playwright and novelist Victor Hugo, a former Royalist turned ardent Republican after 1848, moved to the British island of Guernsey during the Second Empire, and there had the freedom to write the novel considered his masterpiece, *Les Misérables*. Hugo maintained a critical assault through literature, but his physical distance from France also assured his physical safety.

Writers were not always on the margins looking in. The emergence of the novel as a literary form and Realism as its aesthetic made novel-writing the key to the new bourgeois social order. Honoré de Balzac sought to use literature to both chronicle and critique the new France. His monumental project of *La Comédie humaine* with its ninety-five volumes left the writer dead from exhaustion at the age of fifty-one, calling at his deathbed for Dr. Bianchon, a character from his series, to come and save him. The elision of reality and representation also led to such notorious incidents as the obscenity trial of Gustave Flaubert in January 1857. It was not just the adulterous affair at the novel's center that offended contemporary sensibilities: prosecutors claimed that the novel would encourage adulterous behavior in wives. The notion that the male writer could get inside the mind of his protagonist, Emma Bovary, also troubled the prosecution. Flaubert was acquitted but the case is proof of a heightened sense of the continuity between art and life.

Novelists became more and more devoted to documenting their own world. Authors such as Emile Zola began to write in a French which until that time was primarily used only in speech. Zola introduced not only the language of everyday life but also its "argot"—the slang of the working classes. This slang was in and of itself a novelty for bourgeois readers for whom such language allowed them to peer into the lives of those who often merely served them.

The importance of French literature, and the canonical stature of so many French novels from Stendhal to Marcel Proust, cannot be uncoupled from the political importance of France for much of the nineteenth and early twentieth centuries. The belief in the quality of these novels also attached universal excellence to French place and culture. Yet French authors are also responsible for some of the most translated and popular works of literature based in imaginary worlds. During the Old Regime, Charles Perrault's fantastic stories "Puss in Boots," "Cinderella," "Little Red Riding Hood," and "Sleeping Beauty" established the genre of the written fairy tale by introducing peasant tales to a reading public. They are among the most translated, adapted, and retold literary works.

France proved a cradle for futuristic fiction as well. Along with H. G. Wells, Jules Verne is considered one of the founders of science fiction, and his tales featured an international array of globetrotting characters. His novels have sold three times as many as have Shakespeare's plays. Verne's status as a global author is part of a French tradition of thinking in universal terms that made the work so eminently exportable.

If the global concerns of Verne's tales positioned them well for cultural dissemination, it might be fair to say that the planetary concerns of Antoine de Saint-Exupéry's *The Little Prince* (1943) have helped it become one of the most read books of the twentieth century, with more than 80 million copies sold and translations into more than 180 languages. The author, an aristocratic pilot, wrote it during his New York exile from occupied France during World War II. This small book, illustrated by the author's watercolors and aimed simultaneously at adults and children, focuses on the universal themes of love and responsibility cultivated through caring relationships (between the prince and the pilot, the prince and the fox, the prince and his rose).

The narrative unfolds across the entire universe. Set on a series of planets that are merely stars in the great desert where the pilot and the prince meet, it offers lessons about the enormity of the earth and its relative importance in relation to the humans who inhabit it but rarely see it. The story suggests that what is invisible is most important and emphasizes sentimental attachment. Although the disappearance of the prince at the story's end can be thought to teach lessons about loss, the reader is also finally urged to see him or herself as connected not just to people but also to the physical universe itself. The book's final image represents the empty desert, with the prince potentially returned to his planet. Rather than the experience of an exiled man longing for home, Saint-Exupéry instead traces the contours of a world in which we might not see everyone or everything but that we care about it anyway. A universal message produced in a war-torn world, *The Little Prince* is a French-language book that captures the humanistic elements of the French civilizing mission.

Francophonie

Whether read in translation or in French, exemplary works by French authors attest to their broad impact. The complexity of the notion of the civilizing mission, with its dual aspects of imperial arrogance and utopianism, has also resulted in the creation of "Francophonie"—the brainchild, in some measure, of those as touched by the French linguistic obsession and the civilizing mission as the French themselves.

Francophonie is a complex term. A distinction can be made between lower case "f" and capital "f" Francophonie. The term was originally coined in 1880 to refer to the worldwide community of French speakers and clearly became relevant during imperial expansion. As the socialist Jean Jaurès explained in 1884, "Our colonies will only be French in their understanding and their heart when they understand French.... For France above all, language is the necessary instrument of colonization." Today an estimated 200 million people are thought to be "francophone." The term's current use can be attributed to Léopold Sédar Senghor, poet, co-founder of the Negritude movement, and first president of Senegal. In a 1962 issue of the journal *Esprit*, he explained that "'Francophonie is a complete Humanism, weaving its way around the world: a symbiosis of the 'latent energies' of all the continents, of all the races." Senghor envisioned a postcolonial condition in which newly independent countries could use the language as a tool of nationalization. He reasoned that it might give new nations the ability to relate to other countries not only within their own region but also as far-flung as Switzerland, Canada, and Belgium, and the host of other majority French-speaking countries or nations. For him, then, French as a second language would be a choice rather than an imposition. An articulate adherent of the notion of the importance of the French language, he explained, "In the rubble of colonialism, we have found this wonderful tool—the French language."

The term with a capital "F" is also used to denote the International Organization of the Francophonie (OIF), whose most recent title derives from 1998 but which was founded in 1970. Since 1987 the organization has met every two years and consists of fifty-six members, three associate members, and fourteen observers who constitute an international organization of the French-speaking world. Francophonie consists of countries where French is native; countries that have been colonized by France or Belgium; or countries such as Romania and Bulgaria that have chosen affiliation. While some associated members such as Cyprus have only 12 percent French speakers, Algeria, where at least 50 percent of the population speaks French, is not a member for political reasons. One could even say that Algerian independence has been founded on the disestablishment of French, despite its widespread use. The OIF endorses a notion of the French language as liberated from its connection with the nation of France, a notion that in principle makes sense but is also ironically consonant with the way the French approach their language: as a universal one, detached from the physical place of France.

Francophonie also stands for cultural diversity through linguistic pluralism in its adherence to French in the face of the growing dominance of the English language. The organization works, for example, to continue the use of French at the United Nations. France itself initially had a rather chilly relation to francophonie because it smacked of neocolonialism, but since the 1990s the country has become a major player in the organization. This about-face has produced tension as France now presumes that it should play a leading position.

The successes of foreign-born authors writing in French in literary competitions within France has led to another new twist on francophonie. In 2006 such writers won five of the country's major book awards, including the Prix Goncourt, the highest award, which went to New York–born author Jonathan Littell for his Holocaust novel *The Kindly Ones* (*Les Bienveillantes*). Other winners that year hailed from Canada, Congo, and Cameroon. This was not the first time a foreign-born writer had won the Prix Goncourt (for example, in 1987 the Moroccan Tahar Ben Jelloun won), but the particularly rich crop of non-French literary talent writing in French gave inspiration to those who declared they were part of the movement for a "world literature in French." In March 2007, forty-four authors published a manifesto in the newspaper *Le Monde* proclaiming the dissociation of writing in French with France as part of a Copernican moment, by which they meant a moment of radical discovery and breakthrough. They subsequently proclaimed the death of francophonie, "No one speaks francophone, and no one writes francophone. Francophonie is the light of a dead star." They declared that Francophonie was outdated and insisted that where once France functioned as a cultural center, "The center is from now all over, in the four corners of the world." In a celebratory move of post-postcolonial consciousness, the signatories declared that what had been divested was "all powers other than poetry and the imagination, which has only the spirit as its frontiers." The irony of this declaration is that although it may move France beyond the model of *rayonnement culturel* (cultural influence), it sounds awfully like the Enlightenment ideas of the Republic of Letters.

Intellectuals

Because of the importance of the written word and as a result of the many outlets for the publication of ideas, intellectuals have played a special role in French society. In addition, because of the French educational system of elite *grandes écoles* (admission, however, is through a national exam) researchers could compete to be assured a salary for life to function as intellectuals; France has been an ideal breeding ground for them. Although every society has its share of philosophers and thinkers, in modern France intellectuals became part of an engaged, social group. Their activism was known, of course, before the Revolution, especially in the case of Voltaire's defense of the Huguenot Jean Calas, who had been wrongly accused of murdering his son to prevent his conversion to Catholicism. Voltaire's intervention in the case led to a retrial and a reversal of Calas' conviction. Centuries later, when asked why he did not clamp down more on Sartre and his friends' opposition to the government, Charles de Gaulle replied by saying you "do not imprison Voltaire." Much happened between the Calas case and de Gaulle's era; yet when it comes to the social contribution of intellectuals, the Dreyfus Affair played a pivotal role.

The affair revolved around the 1894 accusation and imprisonment of a Jewish army captain Alfred Dreyfus, for spying and treason. There were many inconsistencies in the initial trial and subsequent re-trial. The writer Emile Zola intervened in 1898 when the newspaper *L'Aurore* published his open letter, now known as "J'accuse," denouncing the French Army for a cover-up and the French judicial system for irresponsibility. The following day, the paper printed a "Manifesto of the Intellectuals" in which the group of writers and artists demanded the reopening of the case. The signed petition, in which individuals also claimed a collective identity as intellectuals, helped establish the role of the public intellectual. At the time it unleashed an unprecedented public debate in which artists, writers, academics, and newspapers of all kinds divided into camps of Dreyfusards and anti-Dreyfusards. The former consisted of those who were antiestablishment in general while the latter clung to the authority of the military. Yet the pro-Dreyfus intellectuals also made the case that they had a special role to play because their academic training made them more rational and thus less likely to bend to the will of authority. By virtue of the lively and growing mass press, it seemed all of Paris had chosen a camp.

Zola's involvement triggered a libel trial against him. He was convicted but sought exile in England for a year. The tide of the initial case had, with Zola's help, turned in favor of Dreyfus; Zola returned and was pardoned; Dreyfus was eventually exonerated. The affair is often seen as proof of the overwhelming anti-Semitism in France at the time because so much of the anti-Dreyfus rhetoric and imagery dealt in Jewish stereotypes. It also led the Viennese journalist Theodore Herzel to advocate for Zionism on the grounds that even in the land of liberty, equality, and fraternity, Jews were persecuted. Yet, the system did eventually right the wrong against the defendant while, one could argue, strengthening the French tradition of defending the rights of man in a very public way.

The French press has fashioned a significant role for intellectuals since the affair. For example, the best-known intellectual of the era after World War II, Jean-Paul Sartre, founded *Les Temps modernes*, a journal that propagated the notion of the committed

Surtout ! ne parlons pas de l'affaire Dreyfus !

... Ils en ont parlé...

3. In 1898 Caran d'Ache published this witty cartoon, "A Family Dinner," during the Dreyfus Affair, pointing out the deep and broad divisions in French society due to the Affair. The caption reads: "Especially! Don't talk about the Dreyfus Affair." "They did."

intellectual. In the wake of the street demonstrations for social and cultural reform in May 1968, Sartre also helped to found the left-of-center newspaper *Libération*.

The term "public intellectual" is a form of redundancy in France where books still have an audience, and writers and scholars are asked to opine on matters far from their area of expertise. Academics have their own newspaper columns and also direct series at influential presses. In perhaps one of contemporary mass society's strangest pairings, intellectuals in France have also been a steady presence on television. Books constituted the center of such programs as *Lectures pour tous*, *Apostrophes*, and *Bouillon de culture*.

While French intellectuals reached a broad public at home, such luminaries as Michel Foucault, Jean Baudrillard, and Jacques Derrida also managed to dominate theory in the humanities and social sciences in the 1970s and '80s, both in France and abroad. French culture became associated with complex theory in the highest of academic circles. For scholars, to know French continued to be a key to accessing the most important intellectual trends and theories in addition to an important literary tradition.

If intellectual life became part and parcel of what was "civilized" about France, the wide dissemination of the language did not simply rest on an agenda of required schooling, brilliant prose, and the geopolitical power to force culture down the throats of unequally powerful recipients. France has developed a robust set of outlets for the spread of information in French. For example, in 1841, Charles Havas created the first news agency. Today, known as Agence France Presse, it remains the third largest news agency in the world behind Reuters and the AP. The television network, TV5, a cable channel founded in 1984 that agglomerates the best of French-language programs by repackaging three French-language stations, is a major player in cable television on a global scale.

The dissemination of information from France also helped eventually bring people to France. One of the remarkable achievements of the nineteenth century was that Paris became the most visited place in the world—and that remains the case to this day. The French dedication to visual spectacle has made all roads lead, again, back to Paris. Although Paris took up more than the lion's share of the oeuvre of a writer such as Balzac, the capital city has also played a unique role in constructing the myth of France through images and a sense of place. The power of the French language is fundamental but does not sufficiently explain French influence in the modern world. As the American World War I song asked, "How are you gonna keep 'em down on the farm after they've seen Paree?"

Chapter 3
Paris and magnetic appeal

"Everything is so truly regal, so large, so grand, so comprehensive it makes me jealous." Victoria, the most powerful monarch on the planet and the queen of France's main rival, knew that the French capital offered an incomparable spectacle, even before the government and private speculators had finished shining up its sparkling new boulevards and apartment buildings. The English queen made her comment on the occasion of a visit during the Paris Exposition of 1855, the first of the five (1855, 1867, 1878, 1889, and 1900) that France would host by the time the century ended. The expositions alone helped draw visitors to the French capital. In 1900, a remarkable 51 million people visited Paris during the six-month celebration that dubbed itself the "universal exposition," putting its aspirations and sense of self front and center in its very naming process.

If France had a rich culture of the written word that propagated the importance of the French language, the equal dedication to the production and display of what was regarded as the universal language of images facilitated making the French capital, in particular, an international stage manager of world culture. Visual culture in modern France, from the fine arts to the mass-reproduced commercial forms such as photography, fashion, and film played a central role in creating the magnetic pull toward

Paris. The history of Paris, perhaps like Rome before it, also testifies to the fact that great capitals do not simply embody the nation to its citizens but also advance the nation's significance on a global scale. From art museums and world's fairs to the spoils of empire in its ethnographic museums, Paris became a place to visit in the name of seeing the best of French and world culture on display.

Although all major capitals have magnetic appeal, Paris seems to hold a special place in the pantheon. A battle raged between the power of the countryside, where the majority of the population lived until the twentieth century, and the overwhelming appeal of the capital over the course of modern French history. The banality of the giant presence of Paris has led to the development of a cottage industry of historians working on the provinces, on rural life, and on the colonies. The rich and varied set of histories they have produced guarantee that French history does not rise and fall with the fate of Paris, despite its overwhelming importance.

It is a hard story to modify, for Paris did more than just dictate national life from the center, having transformed the site of the Capetian throne into the seat of the modern Republic. Paris wed the promise of political democracy and the rights of man and the reputation for tolerating foreigners with the glitter and beauty of an internationally oriented cultural capital. This produced an urban mythology that blended all these qualities. Thus Paris also became known as a culturally free and artistically open city, leading the charge with one of the nineteenth century's great battle cries: progress.

Haussmannization

The story of image-making and positive change in Paris begins with the physical reconstruction of the city in the mid-nineteenth century. It reoriented the physical space toward seeing and looking, helping to construct the city itself as a spectacular image. That renovation is often called Haussmannization, named after Baron Georges Haussmann, the Prefect of the Seine under Napoleon III, who directed the planning and execution of the city's modernization. Haussmann's plan soon became the global model for similar urban renovations and planning throughout the world.

Redevelopment began in the 1850s at the city's center with the razing of the medieval pattern of small and irregular streets in the densely populated area around the Cathedral of Notre Dame on the Ile de la Cité. A boulevard would now run through the area—a leitmotif that characterized the process that favored radical change as opposed to minor improvements. Contemporaries joked that Haussmann would have straightened the bends in the Seine River in order to improve the view across his new bridges. With these changes came land speculation and the displacement of vast numbers of working-class Parisians who found themselves forced out of their houses.

Boulevards not only facilitated the circulation of people and goods but also provided sweeping vistas and generally prioritized looking and seeing. The boulevards created a new social geography, which turned the street into a spectacle. What made the spectacle worth seeing was the sense that any and all observers might gather there to watch and be part of the crowd. Alfred Delvau, a nineteenth-century Parisian man-about-town, proclaimed that "the boulevards are not only the heart and head of Paris, but also the soul of the entire world." Even such Parisian boosterism shared the logic of universalism. Among the regime's crowning achievements, not completed until well into the Third Republic in 1876, the new Opéra, designed by Charles Garnier, theatrically staged the audience. It offered a ceremonial staircase as wide as a boulevard and a set of boxes that created a theatrical visual experience, which rivaled the shows the audience came to see and hear.

4. The monumental staircase at the Paris Opéra designed by Charles Garnier during the period of Parisian modernization, like the new boulevards throughout the city, was made for seeing and being seen.

Less showy infrastructure improvements also featured prominently in the city's redesign. Aside from the boulevards, sidewalks were made of improved paving materials such as macadam. The plan also connected the city below ground by magnificent new sewers, an underground pneumatic mail system, and eventually the Métro in 1900. New iron-and-glass pavilions proclaimed the modernity of the redesigned central market, "Les Halles," which Emile Zola dubbed "the belly of Paris" in his eponymous novel. The city even got a new morgue, complete with a plate glass window through which corpses were displayed in the hope that those who had died in the public domain would be identified before their burial. Considered free public theater, the area in front of the building, in the shadows of Notre Dame, teemed with visitors and street vendors selling oranges and candy.

Green spaces also mattered in the new Paris. Napoleon III, the Republican devotee-turned-emperor, having spent his exile from France during the July Monarchy (1830–48) in London, had developed an appreciation for parks, and his plan provided for spaces such as the Bois de Boulogne, the Park Montsouris, and the Buttes Chaumont that fed the lungs of the city.

The size of the city itself more than doubled during the Second Empire, and its population increased by 50 percent as the outer neighborhoods such as Belleville and Ménilmontant were annexed to the city. As Paris was growing larger, such major new monuments to modern life as train stations and department stores appeared as the cathedrals of the nineteenth century, and they welcomed a huge cross-section of the population. Trains were fundamental in bringing the large population of migrants to the French capital. By the end of the Second Empire, France was home to almost 800,000 foreign-born residents, the vast majority of whom lived in Paris. As a busy crossroads, the train station became the symbol, par excellence, of the modern city on the move. It is no wonder that Jacques Offenbach's 1866 comic opera *La Vie parisienne* opens in a train station or that countless painters, Manet among them, painted the cavernous steam-filled spaces. One of the busiest of the nineteenth-century stations, the Gare St. Lazare, literally poured people from the train right into the Galeries Lafayette and Au Printemps, department stores that were built only a few minutes' walk from the station.

Consumerism and display

Although the ubiquity of department stores today may make them seem like natural institutions that must have always been a part of the urban fabric, they are evidence of a new set of assumptions about consumerism that emerged first—and in Paris—in the mid-nineteenth century. These stores derived their economic success from the principle of selling in greater volume than small shops could, with a smaller profit margin at a fixed price. But to achieve that end, they also indulged in some of the most dramatic forms of visual enticement practiced in the century. Among the earliest institutions to use both plate glass and electricity on a consistent basis, they openly solicited any and all comers. The new sumptuous buildings and the arrangement of their products were wonderfully re-created in Zola's novel *The Ladies' Paradise*. "It was like a riot of color, a joy of the street bursting out here, in this wide open shopping corner where everyone could go and feast their eyes," Zola wrote. The department stores were remarkable emporia that not only claimed to put the universe in a garden on permanent display but also would later inspire the logic of the universal expositions. They promised to make all the world's products available to shoppers under one roof; they entranced seemingly powerless female shoppers, and in their wake, doctors began to diagnose new pathologies such as kleptomania.

The nineteenth-century historian Ernest Renan exclaimed that at the expositions, "Europe is off to view the merchandise," which later led the philosopher Walter Benjamin to describe them as pilgrimages to the commodity fetish. The relation between viewing and consumption, aided by the city renovations that prioritized street life as a visual experience, changed the charge of crowd gatherings in Paris since the Revolution from negative to positive. Whether one's aim was to tame it, join it, or please it, the crowd had become a central player in modern France. French political culture had earlier seemed to hinge on the collective action of the Parisian crowd during the Revolution of 1789, again in 1848, and especially in the bloody showdown between the government and the Communards in 1871.

Although Haussmann's renovations have been interpreted as a form of crowd control, it is probably more accurate to say that the capitalist logic of crowd-pleasing through consumerism came to dominate street life in Paris in the second half of the nineteenth century. New forms of street furniture such as the Morris Columns, those advertising structures located on major boulevards, offered dedicated public spaces for advertising posters. This did not prevent the invasion of other city spaces, including the sides of omnibuses and theater curtains, from hosting a new and splashy form of visual culture—the four-color lithographic poster. Far from its early handbill origins with black-and-white, text-laden small pieces of paper, the color poster became the art of the Parisian wall. Poster art, derided by critics as a "mobile and degenerate art form," changed the look of the city, tarting it up and saturating its streets with advertisements. Jules Chéret, known as the master of the poster, who made more than one thousand designs in the 1870s and 1880s, linked bright colors and the unbridled joy of lithe and smiling women with every product from soap to bicycles to liquor to music hall shows.

Paris had always had an important theatrical tradition. Over the course of the nineteenth century, new commercial entertainments—music and dance halls such as the Moulin Rouge in Montmartre and the Folies Bergère down the hill—pioneered a form of variety shows featuring contortionists, cyclists, jugglers, singers, and even the "Pétomane" (farter). These entertainments also revived and popularized the "can-can" or "Chahut"—the dance immortalized in many of the posters of Henri de Toulouse-Lautrec. The can-can included a scandalous display of women's undergarments and an athletic eroticism that made it one of the raciest shows in town. Paris also developed a rich landscape of café-concerts, where popular songs could be heard for the price of a drink or two. These cabaret singers, from Aristide Bruant to Yvette Guilbert, performed narrative tales of their hardscrabble origins and performed street-savvy acts about the tough-luck life for wealthy middle class and foreign audiences who went to hear them as part of an increasing habit of urban slumming.

If consumer culture saturated public space, the expositions and their unprecedented scale, scope, and frequency in Paris

5. A poster by Henri de Toulouse-Lautrec advertises the Moulin Rouge, 1891.

demanded special attention, as they further cemented the tie of consumption to spectacular visual display. Paris, in short, did not merely host expositions, it had become one. Although Paris was not the only city to host world's fairs, it does have the distinction of having hosted the lion's share. The most remembered were held at the end of the century: the one in 1889 gave Paris its iconic object in the Eiffel Tower; the other, in 1900, held the record for the most-visited fair until 1970, when Osaka, Japan, surpassed it.

In choosing to make the world's tallest structure the focus of an event that was planned to celebrate the centennial of the French Revolution, the French commemorated both the grandeur of the Revolution and the forward-thinking aspects of their radical past.

6. The fashionably dressed "Parisienne" atop the monumental Porte Binet at the Universal Exposition, Paris, 1900, attested that contemporary fashion rather than out-of-style allegory dominated the Exposition in 1900.

In 1900 *La Parisienne*, a gigantic statue of "the modern woman" attired in a costume designed by the couturier Paquin, broke with the conventions of monumental sculpture, which tended toward the allegorical or the heroic, and instead advertised style, fashion, and modern life as well as the contemporary decorative arts. The expositions offered a cavalcade of things and experiences, from a display of scientific innovations to pavilions dedicated to the fine arts to an assortment of entertainments such as the "Cairo Street" and "Buffalo Bill's Wild West Show" (both in 1889). Over time, the increasing number of privately funded commercial entertainments offered what might be considered as "infotainment" today. Attractions such as the Maréorama and the Tour du Monde simulated boat and train rides in front of moving panoramas offering a vision of far-flung places that unfolded before the eyes of the spectators. These rides may have been precursors to modern amusement parks, but they also suggest that the appeal of the fair

7. The Moroccan Café on "Cairo Street" epitomized the exoticism of the Universal Exposition of 1889.

and its attractions resided in the experience of exposure to the entire world in condensed version on the fairgrounds.

Museum culture

The expositions also mimicked the general conceit of all great nineteenth-century capital cities whose claims to distinction resided in their scale and ability to offer a digested, condensed array of the human experience. If the expositions took real life and literally transformed it into a show, this experience also had a particular resonance and familiarity in Paris, which had an unparalleled array of museums, most notably the Louvre. Even before the expositions took the world as display to new heights by spectacularizing everyday life in displays dedicated to work or human habitation, Paris had been home for more than a hundred years to the greatest public collection and exhibition of civilization's artistic achievements.

During the revolutionary era, several museums emerged: the Museum of Natural History (from the former Jardin des Plantes), the Conservatory of Arts and Métiers (which displayed new inventions and technological innovation), the Museum of French Monuments, and the Louvre. This last institution, opened during the height of the Revolution in 1793 on the first anniversary of the end of the monarchy, became the world's paradigmatic public art museum. It is still the largest and most visited museum anywhere in the world. The revolutionaries nationalized the king's former palace and his collection of paintings, drawings, sculptures, and other objects, and put them on permanent display, free of charge and open to the public—who were now declared their owners. The collection also included a significant amount of religious art newly confiscated during the Revolution. Its conservation in the Louvre helped assure it a future. Institutions such as the museum replaced religious experience with a secularized aesthetic.

Although the royal collection itself was not particularly dedicated to French art (nationalism in art became more a function of the nineteenth century than of earlier periods), the Napoleonic military campaigns especially enriched the museum's collection. Napoleon brought approximately four hundred treasures from Italy, including the four magnificent bronze horses from St. Mark's Cathedral in Venice. At the end of his regime, some of the plunder was returned, including the horses, which were simply lifted off the top of the Arc du Carrousel by the Germans and sent back to Venice. Rather than appropriate the objects as simple war loot, Napoleon legalized the transfer through written agreements. This great transfer of antiquities helped establish that Paris, rather than Rome, would become the nineteenth-century European cultural capital for the propagation of civilization, a reputation due in no small measure to its visual expression in art and architecture.

The Louvre defined what has been called the "universal survey museum" and continues to exercise enormous influence today. In the twenty-first century, it has been franchised by a 2007 agreement between the government of France and the city of Abu Dhabi. In an agreement worth 1.3 billion dollars to the French, the Louvre will attach its name to a new 260,000-square-foot complex there, designed by French architect Jean Nouvel. The museum direction (as part of a new international agency for French museums) will oversee the building and installation of the institution as part of a leisure complex on Saadiyat Island, opposite the city of Abu Dhabi. (The island will also include a branch of the Guggenheim, presumably for contemporary art.) A direct gift of $32.5 million from Abu Dhabi will also help renovate a new "international wing" of the Louvre in its Parisian headquarters.

The French president at the time of the deal's creation, Jacques Chirac, supported the decision, explaining that "by choosing the Louvre, the emirate of Abu Dhabi not only sealed a partnership with the world's most visited and well-known museum, but selected one which, from its very inception, had a vocation to reach out to the world, to the essence of mankind, through the contemplation of works of art.... Having been originally created from ancient French Royal collections, and constantly enriched over more than two centuries, the Louvre has adhered, from its beginning, to a conviction that art is a universal messenger." Such a grandiose impression has enabled the Louvre to draw visitors to the heart of the French capital for more than two hundred years. Yet the new branch of the Louvre offers a remarkable combination of two models of French culture: the dissemination of the civilizing mission and the magnetic appeal of culture in Paris.

In addition, the rise of travel since the late nineteenth century made Paris a singular tourist destination. More recently, globalization has made shipping cultural objects more common, effectively de-territorializing culture in unpredictable ways. France nevertheless continues to play an important role in such new global equations because of its history as collector and arbiter of world culture.

By the mid-nineteenth century, Paris functioned as the new Rome by virtue of the imperial makeover of Haussmannization and also because every artist sought to visit the Louvre's great collections. The French also cultivated art instruction in an incomparable manner. In particular, the Ecole des Beaux-Arts, founded in 1795, soon became the European center of training for painting and sculpture. The French state created the Academy that ran the school, determined what counted as great art, and then showed and bought the art in large quantities to further enhance its values and the power of its teachers and students. In fact, whatever the political regime, its leaders all agreed that state support of art would enhance the regime. If the World's Fairs were venues for the display of art and industry, the biennial Salon run by the Academy of Fine Arts functioned as the primary institution for the display of contemporary painting. Between 1791 and 1860, seven to eight thousand painters exhibited 68,238 paintings. Hundreds of thousands of visitors frequented the Salon (520,000 in 1876) to see the fortunate artists whose work had been selected for display by the jury. The jury, which initially consisted only of members of the Academy, also rejected thousands of artists, who were thus excluded from the biennial display.

The hermeticism of the Salon system also generated the initial celebrity of the Impressionists, who eventually became the most popular artists in the world. Although there is much debate about what Impressionism is and what it can tell us about the society in which it thrived, there is little dispute that the painters shared a profound hostility to the Academy of Fine Arts and acted on that, as a group, in the 1860s and '70s. Academic painting drew on classical themes, on history and especially antiquity; the Impressionists instead painted modern life. They organized their own exhibitions, especially in the formation of the Independent Salon. Their art challenged regimes of both taste and politics until the Republic was firmly established in the 1870s. From that point on, their art was more consonant with the democracy of the new regime, silencing its work as a form of critique but not lessening its popularity.

Having undermined the Salon, Impressionists helped bolster the emergent system of exhibition in the private art gallery and often exhibited in the new style of one-person shows. Dealers such as Paul Durand-Ruel ascended to power as tastemakers who would now help guide an art-buying public, which had emerged as a force to be pleased. Their world and their interests came to define what was modern about modern art. Art literally depicted the pleasures of a market society and exposed its dark underside. As contemporary Paris increasingly became the actual or implied subject of paintings, its reputation as a center of artistic production and as a place to see only increased. As the century wore on, the newfangled modes of visual expression that were deeply connected to the fabric of modern urban life such as photography, the poster, and film, flourished in the French capital.

Novel technologies of representation

Photography, which made a fledgling appearance in the late 1820s in the experiments of inventor Nicéphore Niépce, became firmly entrenched as a process by Louis Daguerre in 1838. He created the "daguerreotype," a positive image taken directly from the dark chamber of a camera obscura. France declared the invention of photography as a gift to the world in a joint meeting of the Academy of Science and the Academy of Fine Arts in 1839. In exchange, Daguerre and the Niépce's heirs were given pensions for life by the French state. Photography lent credence to a new fantasy of archiving modern urban life as long exposure times favored representations of place. Eventually, the portrait would join landscape as the genres most favored in the new proliferation of images. In addition, photography's limited ability to truthfully capture life as it actually transpired was actively debated then and continues to this day.

Photography nevertheless contributed to the process by which nineteenth-century Parisian life became the stuff of myth through the dissemination of images. Haussmann documented his renovations by hiring Charles Marville to photograph Paris before and after the demolitions. City views already had a rich iconographic tradition in woodcuts, engravings, and lithographs. Photography would soon follow, especially once postcards became widely available in the last decade of the nineteenth century. Postcard series consisted of as many as 10,000 views of the modern city they idealized, including its charming corners of "Old Paris." From the now-well-known images produced by Eugène Atget for the city government to the work of the Surrealist photographers Man Ray and Brassaï to the photojournalists of everyday life Robert Doisneau and Henri Cartier-Bresson, so many views of Paris dispersed by the burgeoning press and published in thematic photographic books of Parisian life reinforced the act of consuming the city as an image. Representing Paris in literature had already become so frequent that Balzac called it the "city of a hundred thousand novels." Paintings and photos also repeated and contributed to the heroic trope that the city was a miraculous miniature version of the world.

By the time narrative sound films became popular in the 1920s and '30s, they developed a slightly different optic on Paris. Steeped more explicitly in the culture of "Paris populaire," the films depicted working-class heroes, taxi drivers, and loose women, and were set in as many garret maids' rooms and shady hotels as glamorous nightclubs and elegant cafés. Even one of the most highly valued international film stars of the era, Maurice Chevalier, had an everyman act, complete with the iconic caps and rolled letter *r*'s, which stood as proof of his birth in the Parisian working-class neighborhood of Ménilmontant.

Photography and the newer medium of film, which had its first public screening in Paris' Salon Indien at the Grand Café in 1895, also became embedded in the urban fabric—not so much for the views taken but for the remarkable saturation of the urban milieu by photo studios and venues for the exhibition of film. From the moment of photography's commercial exploitation, Paris fell under the grip of what was known as "Daguerrotypomanie." By 1850, the city had forty photo studios where Parisians and visitors might have their photo portraits taken. These studios also produced the great photographic fad of the day—the carte de visite—the small card emblazoned with the bearer's image. By the same token, movies were exhibited at the expositions, at the yearly city carnivals known as the "Fêtes foraines," in department stores and eventually in the dedicated movie theaters that ranged from the small neighborhood basement theater to sumptuous picture palaces on the boulevards. In 1911 the Gaumont Palace at the Place Clichy became, with its 3,400 seats, the world's largest movie theater. All major metropolitan centers functioned similarly, of course,

8. When it opened in 1911 the Gaumont Palace on the Place de Clichy was the largest movie theater in the world.

but the French claims to "invention" in the history of photography and film, and the recurrent expositions as sites of photographic and cinematic display as well as their status as photographed and filmed events, probably made Paris one of the most "photogenic" places in the world.

Tourists and expatriates

Tourists flocked to Paris because it welcomed looking. Visitors and immigrants alike came to Paris, propelled by images of the city. As a result, Paris also became home to immigrants and expatriates in search of work, on the one hand, and artistic inspiration and community on the other. This experience became so associated with the city that the characters in such films as *Casablanca* could utter phrases like "We'll always have Paris" and have it resonate widely. The singular role played by Paris among diverse groups of artists, writers, intellectuals, and political dissidents who went there seeking international creative communities has made it a perennial leading edge of multiple cultural movements.

Although privileged travelers always visited Paris in order to perfect the international language of diplomacy that they had learned at home and to contemplate art and history as well as partake in the capital's pleasures, the rise of leisure travel in the twentieth century as part of the emergence of a broader consumer culture in the West resulted in more visits to Paris than elsewhere in the world. If Paris has always been the world's great host, in the twentieth century Americans became its great visitors. Tourism for self-improvement and tourism in pursuit of pleasure blurred increasingly over the course of the twentieth century, making Paris a perfect place to visit because of its reputation for being able to satisfy all such urges from the intellectual to the sensual. Study-abroad programs began to flourish in American universities, and Paris became a top destination in such travel and exchange.

The "Lost Generation" of writers such as Ernest Hemingway, F. Scott Fitzgerald, and John Dos Passos made a Paris period a precursor to achievement for cutting-edge American writers. France provided the distance from which they could better see their own country—a romantic conceit that also helped associate these American writers with the sophistication of Europe. Depressed by the ravages of World War I, they lived partially in exile in France, seeking a better life in Europe, while criticizing the excesses of American life in their writing. Their own excesses also became legendary. Of the summer of 1925 when he met Hemingway in Paris, Fitzgerald described it as "1,000 parties and no work."

Paris also attracted Americans seeking the greater freedom of personal expression they associated with the city. American lesbian writers and artists—notably Natalie Clifford Barney, Djuna Barnes, Gertrude Stein, and Alice Toklas—socialized in salons on the Left Bank. In 1940 Gertrude Stein looked back on the almost forty years she had already spent in Paris to explain, "Paris was where the twentieth century was." Stein was not simply referring to her life in the century but she connected the singular role Paris played in the production of innovative literary modernism.

African American soldiers returning from Paris after World War I described a city with much greater racial equality than what they knew at home. In their wake, African American jazz musicians flooded the French capital in the 1920s and headlined in clubs where the craze for jazz was palpable. The African American performer Josephine Baker became a much-sought-after nightclub act. Although she dressed in banana skirts and indulged in all sorts of self-exoticization as part of her act, the St. Louis–born American, who became a French citizen in 1937, also refused to play segregated theaters in the United States. France also inspired her to make a familial statement against racism by adopting twelve children of different races and national origins. Her "rainbow tribe," as she called them, lived on and off in a château deep in the French countryside of the Dordogne. For Baker, France's social commitment to racial equality meant that she had come home there—even away from the cosmopolitan diversity of the capital.

But Paris also held an appeal for the African American literati, among them Richard Wright and James Baldwin. By the end of the 1920s, the African American writer Claude McKay proclaimed that the "cream of Harlem was in Paris." As African Americans celebrated the freedom they felt in Paris, they also had to confront the racism of the French colonial project. That project also ended up bringing black Africans from a broad diaspora to the French capital, where an important strain of francophone Pan-Africanism would subsequently develop.

Less literary American tourists were at once seeking the great bounty of human civilization that could be found in Paris as well as the specialties of French culture. The American Expeditionary Forces deployed almost 2 million American soldiers during World War I, and, for the first time, ordinary Americans spent significant amounts of time there. During the course of World War II, a wide variety of American soldiers also went to Europe for the first time. After the war, peacetime France welcomed 264,000 American visitors in 1950. This number more than quadrupled by 1970 when Americans accounted for the more than 1.35 million visitors to France. The jet age arrived with a new tourist: the economy-class traveler who had little time and wanted to see all of Europe in ten days' vacation. Paris' Orly airport, the first of the jet-age renovated airports, opened in February 1961 and served as the gateway to the Continent.

Food and fashion

Parisians and French government officials may have envisioned Paris as the storehouse of the world's treasures but they also did not hesitate to see it as the apex of a rich and diverse French culture. One particularly vaunted French expertise was the preparation and serving of food, known throughout the world by the French word "cuisine." The author of the *Physiology of Taste* (1825) Jean-Anthelme Brillat-Savarin, declared that "The destiny of nations turns on how they feed themselves," and this founder of "gastronomy" popularized the idea that only in France had eating become a science. Restaurants were an exclusively Parisian institution from their inception in the 1770s to the middle of the nineteenth century. Because Paris had so many visitors, restaurants began to play a disproportionately important role. As publicly available spaces, cafes and restaurants were open to foreigners while also affording them the chance to get a better view of French "daily life" and to literally savor the pleasures of this strange new world. The restaurant, like so many nineteenth-century Parisian institutions, also benefited from the endless promotional literature generated about the capital, and French food thus became the stuff of sensuous dreams abounding in fantasies of perfect sauces. Promoting food has perhaps been as seminal to the success of French cuisine as the food itself.

French regional cuisine as an idea soon followed as the passion of the automobile age, spurred on by the Michelin rating system and the efforts of food writer Maurice Edmond Sailland, the Prince of Gastronomy, who wrote under the pen name Curnonsky. Americans including Julia Child and Peter Mayle have, in the twentieth century, continued to fuel an anthropological fascination with the French relationship to food in everything from the cultivation of quality ingredients to their careful preparation. Not only has this reputation been a boon to French economic interests but food has also been elevated to the rank of patrimony—as part of the great cultural heritage of France. French wine and champagne are major export industries to this day.

The French obsession with food, perhaps reinforced by daily gustatory rituals such as continuing to shop for fresh bread in a world of prepackaged products, proved international news in the early 1990s as a result of what became known as the "French Paradox," a label first used on the television news magazine *60 Minutes*. The French appeared to consume an unusual amount of sumptuous food such as creamy cheeses and lots of red meat and wine, yet had lower rates of death from heart disease than their American counterparts. Although there are no definitive explanations, the benefits of wine or the lack of French snacking and the commitment to ritualistically eating regular and long meals, are often offered as reasons for the paradox. The French prefer their foods fresh and closer to the source (including a willingness to see a rabbit, head to foot, at the butcher's counter) and are never in a hurry when it comes to food. They also believe that "terroir," the link between food and its soil and traditions of cultivation, gives food its taste. Despite this devotion to the Frenchness of French food, France also has the largest number of McDonald's outlets of any country outside the United States. Contradiction held in productive tension also goes right to the gut.

While tradition may shape eating habits, the spirit of innovation made Paris the world capital of that most ephemeral of cultural forms: fashion. Fashion depends on a world of both seeing and being seen, and the Parisian cauldron of spectacle and display served as a necessary precondition for the lead Paris took in establishing itself as an international center for the fashion industry. Like many of the forms of cultural dominance in the modern period, Paris was given a leg up by the Old Regime monarchy's earlier investment in fashion and the complex but well-organized system of guilds that controlled the production of luxury wear. But in the nineteenth century, fashion became a currency that determined every major city's importance, and none rivaled Paris. The mechanization of production and the democratization of supply, which meant that consumers, over a range of social classes, could get access to new products with relative ease, created both ready-to-wear and a new kind of haute couture. While London cornered the market on tradition in dress, Paris became associated with femininity, elegance, and rapid change. This is why the giant statue of *Parisienne* in contemporary garb at the monumental entry at the Exposition of 1900 made sense to organizers and visitors alike.

The fashion designer emerged during the second half of the nineteenth century as the figure who channeled general trends into something artistic and promoted it as a personal vision. A genealogy of the world's great designers begins in Paris in the nineteenth century with the transplanted Englishman Charles Worth and extends to his employee, Paul Poiret, and from him to Elsa Schiaparelli, Madeleine Vionnet, and Coco Chanel. After

World War II, fashion heralded the recovery of France in part due to Christian Dior's "New Look." After Dior's untimely death, the very young Yves Saint Laurent dominated high fashion by creating ready-to-wear looks; later twentieth-century figures such as Christian Lacroix and Jean-Paul Gaulthier have very much followed in that mold. Despite the current dispersal of sites of clothing production all over the globe, fashion weeks maintain the strong connection between cities and fashion. The contemporary circuit begins in New York, travels to London, then on to Milan, and culminates in its final leg in Paris, suggesting the city still maintains a sort of symbolic power to serve as the capital of this international industry. One of the world's largest luxury groups, LVMH (Louis Vuitton Moët Hennessey) is also based in Paris and draws on the city's reputation for fashion and quality.

The capital of modernism

While Paris clearly established fashion as a modern business, the nineteenth-century critic Charles Baudelaire championed the importance of fashion in aesthetic terms. In his 1863 essay about modern life he made the observation, radical for its time, that fashion plates could be used to understand modern notions of beauty. "Couture culture" shared many of the same concerns as the emergent Modernist avant-garde art world since they were both preoccupied with the tension between originality and reproduction, and the difference in value of the unique work of art and the mass-produced commodity. In this way, Parisian fashion both reflected and contributed to Modernist aesthetics.

In early twentieth-century Modernist cultural circles, Paris served as the movement's unofficial capital for an international coterie of artists. The Belgian poet Henri Michaux explained that the bookstore of Adrienne Monnier "is the homeland of (all) those free spirits who have not found a homeland." Partially because of its reputation as cosmopolitan, the city did, in fact, become more so. Literary Modernism flourished there as Proust and Joyce (who could not get published in Great Britain but was fêted in Paris) experimented with ideas of subjectivity and temporality in their works of fiction. Even the "Futurist Manifesto," by F. T. Marinetti, appeared in the French daily *Le Figaro* in February 1909 before it was actually published in Italy. Culture in Paris thrilled people in search of a cutting edge. There the Russian composer Igor Stravinsky and the choreographer Sergei Diaghilev provoked a near riot in the recently opened Théâtre des Champs Elysées, when the Ballets Russes performed *The Rite of Spring* in 1913. Its dissonant musical score as well as the subject and its representation (a pagan spring rite celebrated with revealing costumes) shocked audiences at the time of its debut. The American Isadora Duncan is also commemorated in one of the sculptures on Antoine Bourdelle's bas-relief on the outside of that theater, in the city which first acclaimed her championing of modern dance.

Dada, Surrealism, and Cubism can be thought of as international artistic movements headquartered in Paris. Pablo Picasso, the Spanish Cubist, made his life in France from the 1920s on. Many of the major painters of the School of Paris—Marc Chagall (Russia), Amedeo Modigliani (Italy), Piet Mondrian (Netherlands), Joan Miró (Spain), Constantin Brancusi (Romania), and Chaim Soutine (Lithuania)—were not born in France but moved to Paris, drawn to its artistic energy. So many of the well-known artists of the interwar years who made Paris their home were born elsewhere: the Surrealist poet Guillaume Apollinaire, great master of French word play, was born in Rome of Italian, Polish, and Russian descent. The avant-garde photographer Man Ray (Emmanuel Radnitzky) was born in Brooklyn but made his career in the city of light. The art dealer Daniel-Henry Kahnweiler, who helped establish the value of the Fauve and Cubist painters, was German-born. Artists gathered for the freedom, for each other, and because there they could contemplate the work of other artists in other media that became of interest to them. Paris provided a lab for artists of many nationalities to generate experiments in culture.

Foreign artists also became part of the artistic establishment and government-sponsored culture. In 1960, the minister of culture André Malraux commissioned Marc Chagall to paint the ceiling of the Paris Opéra, the great jewel in the crown of the city's nineteenth-century renovations and the epicenter of French culture and Parisian social life. Chagall, who had lived out the war in New York, had returned to France and settled, along with Picasso and Matisse, on the Côte d'Azur rather than in Paris. Although some critics balked at the notion that a foreign artist would be given so significant a commission, Chagall himself accepted the job without pay (except for the cost of the materials) as a sign of gratitude to his adopted home. The Russian Jewish artist, a naturalized Frenchman, painted the ceiling in 1964, with a theme that celebrated foreign artists and their influence in France. The mural embedded tributes to Moussorgsky, Stravinsky, Tchaikovsky, Rameau, Mozart, Berlioz, Wagner, Beethoven, Verdi, Ravel, and Debussy, only three of them Frenchmen, against a backdrop of Parisian monuments. There is perhaps no simpler and more symbolically meaningful way to summarize Parisian cosmopolitanism in the arts, under the patronage of the French state, than the installation of the Chagall mural to the ceiling at the Paris Opéra.

Yet the Chagall commission also worked to perpetuate a necessary myth. Cosmopolitanism and universalism wove remarkably fragmentary and diverse experiences and cultures into something singular, making Paris an important place. The devastation caused by the two world wars, and the crisis in conceptions of French grandeur wrought by decolonization and the American century, have made it harder to perpetuate ideas of global coherence in culture. It became even more difficult to advance the idea that any one place could be a world capital for any particular art form let alone the many arts that Paris claimed to organize. The investment in being a world center may seem like the worst form of national chauvinism and expression of cultural superiority, yet the spell of Paris has bewitched more than the city's inhabitants for hundreds of years. Especially in a "flattened" world, we will all still have Paris.

Chapter 4
France stirs up the melting pot

France is a nation of immigrants that lacks a proud poetry about tempest-tossed seekers of golden doors. Although approximately 20 percent of the French population is of immigrant origin (considering at least one grandparent), immigration has had, until the late twentieth century, a marginal impact on French collective identity. At the same time, the influx of immigrants constituted a major demographic fact, resulting from industrial development, imperialism, political persecution, decolonization, and globalization. From the end of the nineteenth century until World War II, France welcomed the greatest number of refugees in the world since the United States closed its doors with exclusion acts and imposed more rigid quotas during the interwar years. French national identity since the Revolution, however, has been forged out of shared mythic origins (helped by schoolbooks that taught about "our ancestors, the Gauls") and rested squarely on the principle that permanent residents needed to assimilate into a decidedly Gallic form of French culture. This myth has begun to be rewritten.

In July 1998, the colors of the tricolor appeared to change from "bleu, blanc, rouge" (blue, white, red) to "black, blanc, beur." (black, white, and the colloquial term for the French-born of Arab descent). The French national soccer team, whose stars offered a dramatic portrait of the diversity of the French people, prevailed in the World Cup at home, winning the championship in its own newly built "Stade de France," located in the heavily immigrant-populated northern suburb of Paris, St. Denis. Names such as Zidane, Djrokaeff, and Karembeu revealed the Algerian, Polish, and New Caledonian origins of some of the great heroes whose victory was fêted with spontaneous and traffic-stopping outbursts of joy on the Champs-Elysées, only days before the official national holiday. This triumph suggested that unity had emerged from the diversity of modern France.

The modern French state has operated with an unflinching sense that difference endangers civic unity, a trope going back to the Revolution's ideal of a unitary republican culture. But that culture has not prevented rationalizations for the differences of status that justified slavery, colonization, and racial laws. Assimilation in France has been driven by the notion that the Republic consisted

9. The multiracial world champion French soccer team sings the national anthem in the Stade de France, July 12, 1998. Their success proved that unity could emerge from multi-ethnic and racial France.

of one people, one language, under one set of laws, which itself was a variation on the French monarchy's idea of the kingdom. The Revolution's disestablishment of Roman Catholicism enfranchised Protestants and Jews as individuals but not the Protestant and Jewish communities. The French state has since maintained a vigilant suspicion of what in French is called "communautarisme," which is used to negatively invoke the drive for the special recognition of religious and ethnic communities that in other societies might simply be called "ethnic pluralism." This particular attitude is also evident in such terms as "discrimination positive" (positive discrimination) to mean what Anglo-Saxon countries label "affirmative action."

Republican education, as it had transformed "peasants into Frenchmen," would provide the mechanism of assimilation. It did not dawn on the host culture that immigrants would not pursue cultural integration into Frenchness as a goal and value in and of itself. For centuries the French monarchy, and then the Republic, had managed to project enough élan that French values and culture signified a measure of civilization to be admired and imitated in nonsubjugated cultures. With a vast empire that, by 1900, stretched from Indochina to the Caribbean, claimed one-third of Africa, and was second in size only to the British, France confidently imagined it could extend its integration through education even in far-flung parts of the empire.

French state record-keeping practices put the investment in the unity of the Republic in concrete form. Since 1872, for example, religion has not appeared as a category on the French census. In order to increase diversity among the student body, early twenty-first century educational reforms at one of the elite institutions of higher education, the Institut d'Etudes des Sciences Politiques, targeted students geographically rather than racially, identifying those from "disadvantaged educational zones." Critics of France say the fear of communautarisme is used to thwart the demands for equality by religious and ethnic minorities.

This French stance has served to integrate European immigrants in France in the nineteenth and twentieth centuries—if by success one means being recognized as French despite familial national origin. For example, few recall that the well-known singer Yves Montand was born Ivo Livi to Italian immigrants; the singer-songwriter Serge Gainsbourg was the son of Jewish Russian immigrants; and the philosopher Henri Bergson was born to Polish Jews. French Jews have also played an important leadership role in the state from Adolphe Crémieux's membership in the government of the Second Republic in the mid-nineteenth century to Léon Blum's serving as prime minister to Robert Badinter's role as minister of justice for the Socialist president François Mitterrand during the 1980s. With such a history of immigration and assimilation, we come to the heart of what might seem contradictory and hypocritical in other countries but is held in productive tension in France.

First waves

The French Revolution ushered in an era in which citizenship and national identity became coterminous. The revolutionaries, in defining the nation, also defined who was outside it as much as who was inside it, and thus rewrote laws of nationality. Under the Old Regime, nationality was based on birthplace in which any person born on soil belonging to the king became his subject. As an attempt to reject the notion of the sovereign's realm (and with the zeal of revolutionaries who believed that the laws and principles of the Revolution fundamentally embodied it and thus could be spread territorially) postrevolutionary law enshrined citizenship by descent, establishing that paternity determined nationality instead. French imperialism, first under Napoleon and later during the height of colonialism under the Third Republic, spread the concept that also clarified that French civil servants born abroad would be French, however removed from France in residential and life experience. As a society becomes increasingly mobile and diverse, the Old Regime policy of birthplace conveying status seems the more open and tolerant policy of the two, especially in light of the Nazi's racist ideology based on descent.

France, unlike other Western nations, faced depopulation during the nineteenth century. This demographic fact produced a favorable attitude to immigration because of a perceived labor shortage. Foreign labor offered vital human power in part because the French peasantry, with a good deal of political capital assured by the 1848 law regarding universal male suffrage, profitably stayed on the land longer than in other countries. By 1889, 3 percent of the French population was foreign-born. Belgian, Italian, and Polish laborers worked in mines, in factories, as part of the war effort during World War I, eventually on auto lines and in domestic work (mostly female). Thus, while we may associate the rise of "guest workers" in Europe with the labor boom of the post–World War II era, French industrialization in the nineteenth century depended on just such a system. In response to the first massive wave of immigration into France in the mid nineteenth century, the French state reversed the course of its modern legal history regarding citizenship in 1851; it adopted birthplace citizenship again with the hope that the state would be able to integrate the children of the newly arrived workers.

European political refugees also arrived in France in the first part of the twentieth century. After Mussolini came to power in Italy, the *fuorusciti* (those who went outside) arrived in large numbers in the southern part of France, especially in Nice and Marseille, and eventually made their way to Paris. The Renault factory employed Russian refugees as workers. Armenian refugees from the Turkish genocide also arrived in the 1920s. Polish workers were recruited by a coalition of steel and industry known as the Société Générale d'Immigration, who provided them near-exploitative labor contracts as well as legal protection in terms of residency in order to retain their labor. As political persecutions in Eastern Europe increased by the end of the nineteenth century, France also became the home of a sizable Jewish population that further grew in response to the application of racial laws in Germany in the 1930s.

The glass half empty

To paint a rosy picture of assimilation would be to represent an incomplete one. Modern French history includes violent eruptions of public anti-Semitism and anti-Islamism, the enactment of the racial laws of the Vichy regime, debate over whether there is a role for Islam in France, and the continued identification of Africans and Asians as immigrants in the land of their own birth. The Dreyfus Affair is emblematic of the complexity of these issues in France. It gave voice to a very public form of racial anti-Semitism, which was unprecedented in how it ran through the mass press. Yet we can also look back at the affair as scandalous, precisely because the defenders of the Republic and notions of the universal idea of "the rights of man" have been singularly triumphant. Dreyfus was, in fact, vindicated. The Jewish Lithuanian-born French philosopher Emmanuel Levinas recounted that his father liked to say, "A country that tears itself apart to defend the honor of a small Jewish captain is somewhere worth going."

This notion offered little comfort, however, to the granddaughter of Alfred Dreyfus who was deported from France during the Vichy Regime and died in Auschwitz at the age of twenty-five. Nor did the vindication of Dreyfus permanently make life easy for the Jews in France. The Vichy government, established in the wake of the French defeat, was not only complicit with the Nazis but also independent in its engagement with legal anti-Semitism during the war. The racial laws imposed on French Jews by the Vichy Regime, beginning in late 1940, mark the only instance in modern French history when race (one was categorized a Jew if three grandparents were Jewish or, if you were married to a Jew, if two grandparents were Jewish) defined and determined status.

Even before the French defeat at the hands of the Germans in June 1940, the French government had sought to stem the flood of eastern European Jewish refugees seeking asylum in France by creating refugee camps. France had approximately 350,000 Jews on the eve of the war, half of whom were foreign-born recent arrivals. Between October 1940 and June 1941, a series of laws known as the "Laws of the Jews" effectively excluded all Jews in France from public life. Jews could not be part of the civil service or the professions or work in industry. Starting in the summer of 1941, the state confiscated Jewish property and increasingly established internment camps for Jews, internal enemies (Austrians and Germans), Communists, and eventually Romany gypsies. Camps such as Drancy and Compiègne in the occupied zone went from being internment camps to being transit camps on the road to the death camps after the German invasion of Russia unleashed the "Final Solution." The government also ordered roundups and deportations, including the arrest in July 1942 of almost 13,000 Jews in Paris, among them 4,000 children who were herded into the bike stadium, the Vélodrome d'Hiver, where they were detained without water and food in the middle of the summer until they were transferred to Drancy.

All that said, almost three quarters of the Jews living in France in 1939, foreign and French, survived the war, and France is now home to Europe's largest Jewish population (approximately 600,000 Jews). The size of the postwar Jewish population in France was augmented by the arrival of a new wave of immigrants from the former French colonies in the Middle East. After Algerian independence in 1962, for example, about 100,000 Jews, who were already French citizens by virtue of the Crémieux Laws, arrived in France, creating, for the first time there, a large influx of Sephardic Jews.

The empire comes home

Jews were not the only arrivals from the former French colonies during the era of decolonization. Postcolonial migration emerged especially in the wake of the wars of decolonization, marked by the

French defeat at Dien Bien Phu in 1954. The experience of migrants in France stems from the very variable French colonial policy in regard to citizenship and other French laws about rights and privileges in the colonies. French political decision-makers thought some groups in the colonies were better suited to assimilation than others. One of the first acts of the Government of National Defense in 1870 had been to give full rights of French citizenship to the Jews residing in Algeria. They saw the Jewish population there as fundamentally modern as opposed to the Islamic Algerian culture, whose tribal and nomadic traditions they interpreted as "primitive" and incapable of conveying political subjectivity. French colonialism thus created new hierarchies within the colonies: Jews versus Muslims; the Kabyle (Berber)-speaking versus the Arabs of Algeria.

French colonialists doubted the ability of Muslim Arabs to assimilate because of the important role Islam played in civic life. Until 1946, Muslims were subjects rather than citizens in French Algeria and were governed for the most part by their own indigenous Islamic law. Muslims could seek French citizenship if they were willing to sign away the right to be governed by Muslim law, which constituted a fundamental rejection of Islam. By 1937, only 2,500 Algerians had asked for citizenship through this mechanism. By 1962, only 7000 Muslims had become naturalized French citizens. In 1931, Léon Blum, then a leftist deputy from Narbonne, and Maurice Viollette, an ex-governor general of Algeria, took up the possible expansion of political rights to the indigenous male Algerian elite without affecting their personal Muslim status. By this point, native troops had contributed a great deal to the war effort between 1914 and 1918 (in fact, the Paris mosque was built in 1922 in honor of the sacrifices of North African troops during the war). The year 1931 was also, not coincidentally, when the Colonial Exposition opened in the Bois de Vincennes on the eastern edge of Paris as a display of French imperial élan. Not long thereafter, in 1936 Blum, as prime minister, announced the promotion of almost 21,000 Algerians to citizenship without any consideration of granting independence to Algeria. The white colonials of French origin residing in Algeria, who made it France's largest settler colony, completely rejected the proposal.

Colonial expansion began to abate in the 1930s. In the period after World War II, independence—rather than the fair application French rights—would emerge as the singular battle cry within the colonies. In the wake of Nazism, especially, it became harder to defend the idea of the inherent superiority of European civilization or of any one culture over another. The United Nations, after the war, declared the right to self-determination for all peoples. In a newfangled continuation of colonial ties that seemed to respond to changing circumstances, the new Fourth French Republic created the "Union française" comprising the French colonies.

Yet anticolonial uprisings marked the postwar era. Displays of anti-colonial sentiment in Algeria upon the celebration of the Nazi defeat in 1945 resulting in the Sétif massacre, the French loss at Dien Bien Phu in Indochina in 1954, and the violent war in Algeria that lasted from 1954 to 1962 also included violence at home in France, such as the notorious massacre of innocents at a protest in Paris (November 17, 1961) against the imposition of a curfew on Algerians living there. France eventually lost all its colonies except Guadeloupe, Martinique, Réunion, and French Guiana, all of which remain French to this day.

The empire came home after decolonization in ways that have fundamentally structured and shaped life in France ever since. A new wave of immigrants arrived in the wake of independence, especially from northern and western Africa. As a result, Islam is now the second largest religion in France, with estimates of between 3.7 and 5 million people of Muslim origin or faith, making France home to the largest Muslim population in Europe. Postwar immigration has changed the face of the French Republic and challenged its vision of itself as unitary in ways made palpable by ethnic, national, and racial differences.

Before the war, the vast majority of immigrants from North Africa primarily consisted of Berber men who replaced European immigrants in positions of unskilled labor. After the war, French industry sought out more Algerian workers because they were considered better integrated into French culture (being Francophone) than were Italians or Poles. In 1947 a new law allowed the open circulation of laborers between Algeria and France. Between 1946 and the start of the Algerian war, approximately 200,000 Algerians came to France to look for work. Between Algerian independence, as well as that of Morocco and Tunisia, and the Suez Crisis in 1956, more than 1.2 million people arrived in France from North Africa. The majority were French, even if they had never lived in France. Algeria and Tunisia also had a significant population of Italian descent that repatriated to France rather than to Italy since they were French-speaking and saw greater economic opportunity in France. Tens of thousands of so-called "harkis," Muslim Algerians who served in special French auxiliary military units during the Algerian war, also sought refuge in France, where their reception was not always warm either from the French of European origin or among those of Algerian descent. Unlike the "evolués" (the assimilated French-speaking Algerian Muslims), the "harkis" were indistinguishable from most of the Algerian population, but for their lack of support for the FLN (the victorious Algerian party that led the struggle for independence).

The French government organized and supported immigration with a new system of work permits, given in ten-year increments, which were intended to help develop a path toward citizenship based on work and residency. France sought workers in heavy industry (mining and the automobile industry) as it had a hundred years earlier. During the post–World War II era, aside from North Africans, more than three-quarters of a million Portuguese citizens arrived in France, often clandestinely. Two significant Indochinese migrations occurred—the first around 1954, and the second—the "boat people"—in the 1970s. During that period, African families were reunited when women and children joined the male laborers who constituted the initial postwar wave.

The constriction of the economy beginning in the 1970s, and the particular shift in the labor market away from unskilled and skilled physical labor to tourism and hospitality, created disproportionate unemployment among immigrants. Whether unemployed or employed in low-paying jobs, Portuguese and North African immigrant poverty could be observed in ghettoization, as it had in the nineteenth century when working-class neighborhoods developed in Paris in the newly annexed suburbs of Belleville and in the areas around train stations.

The arrival of immigrants after the war also coincided with a housing crisis in France. In order to eviscerate the growing number of shantytowns that popped up and demarcated the boundaries between large cities and their outskirts, the French government built new apartment buildings in the city as well as housing complexes in industrial suburbs such as Sarcelles, ten miles from central Paris. Government action stepped up after June 1970 when five African workers died of asphyxiation from fumes from a fire in one of the shanties in Aubervilliers, just a few miles northeast of Paris. Known as "cités," the new housing segregated immigrant communities from French-born ones and helped them to develop a shared identity, a shared colloquial French language, and residential experiences. These have been described in literature and film, for example, in Christiane de Rochefort's *Les Petits enfants du siècle* (1961) about French working-class life in subsidized housing in Bagnolet: here mothers produce children to get government financial support. As a pregnant woman pats her stomach, she says, "Here's my refrigerator"—a luxury she will be able to buy with the money she collects from the government for having another baby. More than thirty years later, Mathieu Kassovitz's film *La Haine* (1995) depicts disenfranchised teenage young men in the suburban housing complexes. The film updates the tale of working-class misery with a multicultural set of protagonists who share a common marginalization in French society due as much to race as to class. Such segregation has become a practical form of the "communautarisme" that the French Republic decries.

Of course, as the economy contracted after a remarkable three decades of growth from 1945 to 1975 ("Les Trentes Glorieuses"), whatever covert postcolonial racism existed as a practice was articulated as an ideology and political program of the French National Front, led by Jean-Marie Le Pen. He believes that the culture of former colonial subjects who are now immigrants is incompatible with French life. Le Pen is the most recent incarnation of right-wing xenophobia that used to take its most virulent form in organized anti-Semitism, such as that exhibited during the Dreyfus Affair. The height of Le Pen's power came during the 2002 presidential elections when he received more votes in the first round than did Lionel Jospin, the left candidate. Le Pen earned the right to face Jacques Chirac, the incumbent president, in the second round. Protests against Le Pen's racist extremism began the night he earned the runoff and thus delivered Chirac 82 percent of the vote, one of the biggest landslides in French electoral history. In such moments of clear choice between racism and the values of the rights of man, the French dramatically and emphatically choose the values of the Republic. These may be easy moments of unambiguous choice, but such moments also help perpetuate the unity of the Republic in ways that few modern democratic nations have the privilege to see crystallized except in times of war.

The significant issue for France now is not as much the fate of new arrivals as the integration of those who have already arrived. The rate of immigration to France since the 1980s has slowed relative to other European countries. Tighter legislation about entry, in the form of the anti-immigration Pasqua laws of 1993, has discouraged immigration while creating a new and vital realm of undocumented workers known as the "sans-papiers" (without papers). Although many North African immigrants may have initially harbored a dream of returning home, the reality is that the vast majority have stayed in France, growing from 28 percent of the foreign population in France in 1975 to 39 percent in 1990. Where once the plight of immigrants gave voice to social outrage at poor living conditions, the discussion has turned to whether the new immigrants can actually become integrated members of French society more generally.

When François Mitterrand was elected in 1981, his government sought to improve social services to immigrants, to reform the nationality code, and to grant amnesty to undocumented immigrants in order to create greater loyalty to France. The government met new and organized challenges from the now adult second-generation children of immigrants, known as "beurs" (a colloquial term for French-born children of Arab North African descent), who sought integration into French society and demanded justice in response to acts of racial discrimination. The organization, SOS Racisme, emerged from this period of social protest with a brand of French multiculturalism. The energy behind that organization waned by the end of the 1980s. That moment also produced the government's founding of the Institut du Monde Arabe as a secular institution dedicated to illuminating Franco-Arab relations in a spectacular architectural setting on the banks of the Seine, as if to declare that France accepted that Arab culture was indeed a part of French culture.

The peculiar French politics of multiculturalism

Discussions about social class and economic disenfranchisement shifted to those about cultural identity and racial discrimination after the 1980s. The facts of demography made clear that the number of French-born children of parents born elsewhere was increasing, especially by virtue of a differential birth rate between Muslims and non-Muslims in France. French Muslims may over the course of the twenty-first century constitute closer to one-quarter than one-tenth of the population of France. These changes and tensions also form the background history for the wild celebrations of France's multicultural World Cup–winning soccer team as proof that the new face of France could be multiracial and also strong.

The extreme focus on cultural difference has made discussion about Arab immigrants turn into conversations about Muslims in France. Much of this discussion began in the Republican schools that had played a key role in constructing national identity in a secular Republic. The schools have, in effect, a history of religious intolerance—to Roman Catholicism, that is. In fact, in January 1994, in the midst of ongoing controversies that began in 1989 in the northern French town of Creil where three middle-school girls were expelled for wearing headscarves, nearly 1 million protestors took to the streets of Paris in defense of secular education against the new right-wing government of Edouard Balladur. His intention was to subsidize Catholic education, which led to protest from secularists. At the same time, the "headscarf affair" eventually led to the appointment of a national commission to examine the question of religion in the schools from the Muslim angle. At the end of 2003 the Stasi Commission ruled against the wearing of obvious religious symbols such as large crosses, yarmulkes, and the headscarf in the name of their mission to assure sexual equality and secularism in the public sphere.

The decision has continued to provoke debate rather than settle it, in part because of political changes within France and across the world. What is most dramatic about the period from 1989 when the publication of Salman Rushdie's novel *The Satanic Verses* provoked a declaration of a call for his public execution in Iran to beyond the attacks of September 11, 2001, is an awareness and fear of the rise of Islamic fundamentalism. This development is itself a product of an international context of the new form of deterritorialized political communities developed by the Internet.

Within France, the threat of Islamic fundamentalism must also be set in relation to new public discussion about sexual equality, especially in the wake of the adoption of the law on *parité* (equality) in 2000, which has resulted in slates of candidates needing to have equal representation of men and women in French elections. In a Republic that had denied women the vote until 1944, some wondered about the opportunism of the newfound feminism of the French state and its rejection of the veil in the name of guaranteeing women's equality. Opponents of the veil have been inspired by the rhetoric of *parité*, arguing that the veil amounts to a potent symbol of women's domination in Islam. Still others have suggested that wearing the veil allows young women to assert control over their self-presentation.

Whether gender discrimination is a genuine or opportunistic concern in debates about the veil, there is no doubt that such controversies transpired across Europe at the turn of the twenty-first century. With the largest Muslim population in Europe, France is necessarily a key site for understanding the future of multicultural Europe as well as the meaning of transnational fundamentalist Islamic identity within it. The French Muslim connection is particular. Many Muslims in France originally came from French colonies, and the French government has not been particularly repentant about its imperial past. The French state also continues to have an unusually large stake in wielding influence in the Middle East, a region that remains a center of Francophonie, making any rise in a Pan-Islamic identity of great importance to France.

Unemployment, racial discrimination, and social marginalization underscored by housing segregation are the breeding grounds for a resurgence of Islamic fundamentalism as it can be used to provide both a positive identity and an alternate program for the future. In particular, economic stagnation in France disproportionately affects those of immigrant origins as the increased lack of economic mobility traps them in the lowest social conditions. The riots that began in the Parisian suburbs in October 2005 suggest the complex overlap between economic disenfranchisement and racial discrimination. The riots were triggered by the accidental death of two French-born teenage boys in Clichy-sous-Bois; chased by the police, they were electrocuted when they broke into a fenced-off area that held a power transformer. People living in impoverished neighborhoods broke out in violent protest around France. They burned cars and participated in other forms of civilian unrest, not unlike the race riots that Britain and the United States had witnessed in the 1960s, but that France had largely avoided in the period marked instead by student riots of May 1968. When the then minister of the interior Nicolas Sarkozy called in the imams to help quell the rioters, their ineffectiveness suggested that the situation had little to do with Muslim identity.

The mixed response to the Stasi Commission report on the veil among the Muslim community and the riots in 2005 suggest there is no one French Muslim community. In fact, only in 2003 did an organization come to exist to "represent" the Muslims of France: the *Conseil français du culte musulman* (French council of the Muslim religion), which has become the spokesgroup of the community. This group vies for adherents with other groups, such as the more militantly fundamentalist *Union des organizations islamiques de France* (Union of French Islamic organizations) led by Fouad Alaoui. The increased connection between the Muslims living in France and the French state came as the government grasped that 90 percent of imams in France were born and trained elsewhere, making them potentially unequipped to understand the specificities of life in France; indeed, some of them were simultaneously linked to radical forms of Islam that had their bases outside of France.

The increasingly important role of politicized Islam in French Muslim life and the new focus on it in the media has been fomented in part by the wars in Iraq and Afghanistan, and the lack of peace between Israel and the Palestinians. In particular, while French Christian anti-Semitism is on the wane, vandalism and violence perpetrated by Muslims against Jews in France has increased, from the bombing of the synagogue on the rue Copérnic in 1980 to more recent desecrations of French Jewish schools. Although France acted as an early ally to the Jewish state from 1948 to 1967, after the Six-Day War, most French presidents have trod a careful course, aligned mostly with the Arab states. The exceptional visit of François Mitterrand to Israel in 1982, when he masterfully spoke some Hebrew and explained his support for a Palestinian state, crystallizes what has been the French position, especially in its autonomy from the United States' position in the Middle East.

Yet the focus on what seems like a movement of increasing Islamization masks another powerful reality of those French Muslims who constitute one-third of all Muslims living in Europe: their embrace of French Republican values. It is believed that at least one-half to three-fifths of French Muslims are French citizens; the linguistic enforcement in France is so stringent that immigrants in France speak French, which helps produce social integration. When asked whether they identified as Muslim first and French second, only 46 percent responded yes as opposed to 81 percent of Muslims in Britain. French students of Muslim immigrant origin do no worse in school than their non-Muslim schoolmates in poor school districts. According to a poll conducted by the official French polling agency, the CSA, 90 percent of Muslim respondents in 2004 say they favored gender equality, and 78 percent of French Muslims believe Islam is compatible with Republicanism.

Muslims in France do not appear to show profound Pan-Islamic consciousness. For example, when two French journalists were kidnapped in Iraq in 2004 and the hostage-takers demanded the repeal of the headscarf ban, French Muslims supported the government's rejection of the terrorists' demands. (The journalists were eventually released, but it is unclear whether any concessions were actually made.) There is no perceptible Muslim "vote" in France. Further, the extreme Left, anti-Israel "Euro-Palestine" list, which campaigned in European Union parliamentary elections, received only 10 percent of the vote in France, even in districts where 40 percent of the voters were Muslim. There has been little Muslim presence, however, among the elected members of the French Parliament. Azouz Begag was the first minister of equal opportunity appointed in 2005 under the Villepin government, but he resigned in 2007.

Islam *of* France

In the end, history is producing an Islam *of* France versus simply accounting for the history of Islam *in* France. The early twenty-first century re-Islamization of a certain part of the French Muslim population has provoked renewed conflict and concern that is often met with inflated rhetoric about the indivisibility of the French Republic. It is with practical measures that bridge the economic and social gaps between the French children of recent waves of immigrants and other French people, and probably with more visible symbols such as the national soccer team, that France will remake its cultural bouillon. Modern France, where peasants were once "turned into Frenchmen," will sustain its singular identity while adapting to the changes resulting from its most recent flux of migrations in the period of World War II. Whatever one's creed, such shared experiences as the support of a national sports team, and the production and consumption of musical and cinematic language, creates community and defines French identity among residents of France. The conception of a unitary French state dedicated to advancing an idea of "humanity" while effectively integrating difference remains one of the singular challenges and missions of modern France.

Chapter 5

France hurtles into the future

Although the Eiffel Tower now seems a nostalgic icon of the nineteenth century, at its construction it looked forward while looking back. When it first came to dominate the Parisian landscape in the spring of 1889, France was about to celebrate the one-hundredth anniversary of the French Revolution. For the Republican government, firmly in control after the trials of reestablishing democracy in the wake of the defeat of the Second Empire in the Franco-Prussian War, the tower's importance as a symbol of progress cannot be underestimated

First proposed as a major feature of the Exposition of 1889, it caused a sensation in its own time as the tallest structure in the world and as a milestone in iron construction. Although the idea to build a one-thousand-foot (300-m) tower had circulated earlier in the century, several short-term factors facilitated the realization of Gustave Eiffel's project. First, the expositions held in Europe and America from the mid-nineteenth century on created the context for spectacular and symbolic architectural construction as a form of competition between nations. Second, the snail-paced construction of the granite Washington Monument, begun in 1848 and completed only in 1885, taught the French a lesson, and they decided that building with new materials and doing much of the building "off-site" by using prefabricated iron would make it possible to build quickly. Third, the newly solidified Third French Republic embraced the notion that its construction in iron would demonstrate to the world the merits of a century devoted to rationality and scientific progress in the wake of the French Revolution. As the editor of a popular scientific magazine put it, it would be the "arc de Triomphe of science and industry."

The Eiffel Tower inevitably had its critics, including a group of well-respected mainstream French artists, writers, and intellectuals who complained in 1887, when the plan was first proposed, that it would be a monstrous symbol of the craven machine age that would destroy both the values and image of the world's most important city. Yet it was the engineer himself (an astute businessman and self-promoter) whose vision prevailed. Eiffel not only oversaw a complex manufacturing and building project that was without peer at the time, earned a substantial government commission, and raised construction money by selling stock to investors; he also secured himself a twenty-year guarantee to the profits from the various concessions (restaurants, a theater, souvenir stands), guaranteeing that the tower, built only for a temporary exhibition, would last at least for those twenty years.

While there were many other towers, until the mid-nineteenth century most architecture that reached skyward had been devoted to God. The construction of the Eiffel Tower anticipated the more profane attempts to reach the heavens that would soon find form in the skyscrapers of the United States. Its wide base and narrow tip, and its open latticework of iron to stabilize it against wind, gave the building an originality; it could not, however, be considered a prototype for any other building form. In that way, it is not the "first" skyscraper. Although Eiffel proposed that the tower would be used for scientific experimentation and in more practical domains such as telegraphic communication and observations concerning the weather as well as a great lighting beacon, in practice the tower served little purpose other than to be seen and visited.

Almost 2 million exposition visitors climbed the tower between May and November 1889, and all of the 28–32 million visitors to the exposition laid eyes on it. The novel quality of the facilities on the tower made the ascent worthwhile. The tower had elevators as well as stairs; a number of restaurants, toilets, souvenir stands, even a theater, mailboxes, and its own "newspaper," *Le Figaro de la Tour*. It was at once an engineering feat, a major moment in the history of the creation of tourist attractions, and a celebration of French commitment to the future.

The fact that the Revolution would be commemorated with a symbol for the future makes perfect sense. Although the French attachment to their history and their rootedness in the geography that eventually became the French state has sometimes contributed to the notion that "frenchness" seems to belie modern thinking, the French Republic has been decisively interested in looking forward. Time was effectively reborn when the French stopped the clock on the Old Regime and literally began time anew with the introduction of the Revolutionary calendar in 1793: the months were renamed according to nature and numbered more rationally, beginning from the moment the Assembly declared the Republic in September 1792.

The same Exposition of 1889 not only featured the Eiffel Tower but also the enormous "Gallery of Machines," whose building constituted the largest single-span structure in the world (364 feet long), and where steam-powered machines and elevators were displayed in a building completely lighted by electricity. Opposite the tower stood lighted fountains, one of which featured a statue, *France Lighting the World*. Enlightenment and electricity were paired in France in ways that help explain why the capital became known as the *Ville-Lumière* (the City of Light). The term in French for the Enlightenment (as well as for lights) is "Les

Lumières." The application of technological thinking and a French commitment to notions of progress and the future were expressed in many ways: around dwellings and in urban planning, in the design of transport, and in the rise of consumer culture, leisure, and communication technologies.

Contrary to the image of France as a country solely dedicated to tradition, artisanal craft, and small-scale luxury production, to the countryside and to more recent ideas such as slow food, France has been at the cutting edge of mass production and the development and applications made possible by the high-tech world. In fact, France innovated in technology, in mass culture and consumption, and has contributed much to both dreaming up visions of the future and in making some of those dreams real. In the history of consumerism, such institutions as the department store (the Bon Marché) and the chain grocery store (Félix Potin) were first developed in France. France played a vital role in mechanization from the first guns made of interchangeable parts to the precision rivets that made it possible to assemble the Eiffel Tower so quickly to Renault's making the first automobiles that did not look like motorized carriages. France also defined a path in which technical knowledge was elevated as a form of respectable expert knowledge in a way that has resulted in a society attached to and engaged with both technology itself and with the future as a concept.

The idea that France has a special struggle with modernization has been confused with French resistance to American domination. When decoupled, we can see that France has played an important role in the development of ideas about the future and the application of the technological and engineering skills to make it happen. In fact, if there is something peculiarly French about all this, it is that the French government and individual French people might be characterized as the avant-garde of the avant-garde—devising big utopian schemes, huge marvels such as the renovated sewers in nineteenth century Paris or the Eiffel

Tower, and high-end, high-tech inventions such as supersonic transportation in the twentieth century.

Enlightenment

Technological innovation in modern France is connected to both the set of ideas known as the Enlightenment, which preceded the French Revolution, and the Industrial Revolution that followed it. The Enlightenment put a positive value on practical knowledge, which was codified in France, in particular, by the enormous publication project of the *Encyclopédie*, edited by Denis Diderot and Jean d'Alembert between 1751 and 1772. Although the project sought to give a new shape and structure to all knowledge, it can be distinguished by its emphasis on technology, and its attempt to contextualize and systematize forms of knowledge that had largely been transmitted only through practice and craft. A large proportion of the approximately three thousand images in eleven volumes of illustration dealt with technology or helped describe what at the time was known as the "mechanical arts." Even the originality of linking image and text in this publication project is testament to an interest in the lessons related to concrete things rather than to abstract ideas. The *Encyclopédie* sought to communicate knowledge, usually transmitted socially via studios and workshops, through books instead, elevating practical knowledge to something worth codifying in print.

The Enlightenment and the French Revolution have been linked in terms of abstract ideas about democracy, but they are also connected in the sphere of technical knowledge, from the creation of the metric system to the advances in weaponry made during the revolutionary wars. The Industrial Revolution that followed the political changes of the turn of the nineteenth century also made a lasting impact in France. Steam-driven machinery, factory production, and the emergence of a self-conscious, wage-earning, working class unleashed a set of changes, often first associated with England and then unleashed across the Continent. These changes developed unevenly and had an enormous impact upon social life, not the least of which was a heightened awareness of the power of rapid change.

Industrialization's dreamers

As the social order based on industrialization took hold, increasingly rent asunder by the divisions between capitalists who owned wealth and their exploited employees, such French thinkers as Henri de Saint-Simon and Charles Fourier played key roles as dreamers for the new social order, which became articulated as some of the earliest Socialist visions for the reorganization of society. They were also deeply attached to ideas of progress and to working toward a more perfect future. Like Robert Owen, the Welsh founder of British socialism, Saint-Simon and Fourier put work at the center of the "industrial" society (a term coined by Saint-Simon). Unlike those responsible for the French Revolution who had already shown what the power of the government mobilization of the economy could do in solving food problems and creating the world's largest well-armed standing army, Saint-Simon prioritized the role that scientists, engineers, artists, and industrialists would play in reorganizing communal life.

Saint-Simon's ideas also inspired women to make social and political demands. Jeanne Deroin, a seamstress, helped to found a feminist newspaper, *La Femme Libre*, in 1832. Along with the activist Flora Tristan, they sought suffrage for women and improvements in wages for labor and challenged such bourgeois conventions as marriage.

Many of these proto-socialists shared the idea that work should be oriented toward the common good rather than be defined by the pursuit of selfish interest. Such thinkers as Auguste Comte, the "father of Positivism," sought precise or "positive" social laws. Human society, he argued, had progressed away from the primitive stage, dependent on religious explanation and priests.

Dedicated engineers and technocrats would manage a new order. Those state engineers eventually helped build the infrastructural nation, reconciling the social and technical orders. They had already been tied to the state under the Old Regime that founded the Ecole des Ponts et Chausées (Bridges and Roads) in 1747 and the Ecole des Mines in 1783 in order to provide engineers for the king's many building projects. Society became imagined along the lines of an idealized machine or factory. Before this model became the order of the day, such visions were also prophetically imagined in France where the sense that the future could be better and brighter definitely took hold in the wake of the French and Industrial revolutions.

Many of the new visions had a spatial dimension, suggesting that the social reorganization of people needed to take expression in physical communities. In Great Britain, Robert Owen bought a cotton mill in New Lanark, Scotland, in 1800 and set up a model factory town that mandated only ten hours a day of work per laborer (vs. sometimes as many as seventeen), no corporal punishment, health care, schools and housing. Fourier envisioned a world in which people lived in a large collective building known as a phalanstery, "a building as perfect as the terrain permits," which was to function as an economically harmonious institution. Part agricultural commune, part garden city, the community would insure that each person would work in positions for which they were best suited, and children would live together rather than with their parents. The dreamer Etienne Cabet, who first used the term "communist," described an idealized world in his 1840 novel *Travels in Icaria*. Here, an elected dictatorship organized work, and a visionary city of the future eliminated both private property and money. Thinking about social reform not long afterward became redefined by the powerful insights and observations of two Germans, Friedrich Engels and Karl Marx, who met when they were both living in Paris. For them, the history of France would come to determine their developing laws of social development and transformation.

If Cabet was part social reformer, his Utopian novel also shares some of the visionary and future-oriented perspective that we associate with science fiction, a genre whose origins are not exactly clear but whose best-selling practitioner in the nineteenth century remains one of the most translated authors: the Frenchman Jules Verne. Poised somewhere between adventure and science fiction, Verne based his tales on scientific and technological discoveries of the era in which he lived and thus was as much a commentator on his own world as he was a prognosticator. Verne's writing consisted of fifty-four published stories written between 1863 and 1905 known as the "Voyages Extraordinaires." Verne popularized and built on his own moment of technological change: steamships, the telegraph, trains, and canal digging to offer readers a world of mobility and novelty. He hoped in the process the novels would teach science and geography through fiction. Verne immersed himself in reading the scientific and technological news of the day and relied on family who were experts in math and science to check his work. The stories spin visions of life in the future: travel to the moon, submarines, and journeys to the center of the earth. In an unpublished manuscript written at the start of his career, he even envisioned a Paris in 1960 in which there are machines resembling faxes and in which people travel by automobile and elevated train (all of which did indeed come to pass, while the novel itself did not see the light of day because his editor thought Verne's vision was too somber). In Verne's world, machines take advantage of nature but do not exploit humans.

The idea of a mobile society can be found not only in Verne's obsession with transport technologies and information across distances but also in the fact that his protagonists and scenarios were mostly not located in or living in France. Thus, in *Journey to the Center of the Earth*, the hero is a Danish professor who descends into an Icelandic volcano; Captain Nemo from *20,000 Leagues Under the Sea* is a Europeanized Indian prince trawling around the Atlantic Ocean in a deluxe luxurious submarine; Phileas Fogg, the protagonist of *Around the World in Eighty Days*, is a fabulously funny send-up of British blasé and national stereotypes. The novels ground readers who are then simultaneously unmoored as they read fiction that is more about going places than actually being there. Verne's descriptions linger on modes of transport and the problem of the race against the clock rather than dwell, travelogue-style, on the places journeyed. Positive perspectives of the present as futuristic abound in this most popular of French fiction writers.

Making dreams concrete

French fantasy visions of the future and other, better worlds have also taken concrete form since industrialization. Urban planning and design became a primary means through which a French vision of a tamed and positive technological society took hold. Distinct from the British Arts and Crafts movement, which suggested a more conflicted relationship to industrialization through its emphasis on craftsmanship and its Gothic revivalism, France's engineering forms of iron, steel, and glass could and did wipe away the prevalence of historicism in architecture. Such planners as Tony Garnier, the city architect of Lyon, saw in concrete the possibility of social improvement. He developed the idea of "the industrial city" and published a treatise with that title in 1918. The city of Lyon today bears the mark of this architect dedicated to the functionalism of reinforced concrete, but more significantly, such visions of a spare urban future became well known in France, especially through the Swiss-born planner Charles-Edouard Jeanneret, who took the name Le Corbusier.

Le Corbusier participated in the promotion of modern art and design in France. He joined Amédée Ozenfant and Fernand Léger in founding the journal *L'Esprit Nouveau* that advanced ideas about the harmony between art and science. In his hands, houses became machines for living in. Influenced by his early employer, Auguste Perret, himself an adherent of the use of new building materials and the development of more verticality in city planning, Le Corbusier envisioned a city in which towers dedicated to business would sit at the heart of a redesigned urban agglomeration organized around the free flow of traffic. In that way, Le Corbusier shared Haussmann's nineteenth-century dedication to the flow of traffic, although one can perhaps detect in his preference for the vertical axis an adaptation to the arrival of the car in the city.

He debuted his ideas about urbanism in the 1922 "Contemporary City" project as part of the Autumn Salon, the avant-garde yearly art show. Rather than propose suburbanization, Le Corbusier, in his even more radical Voisin plan, designed for the 1925 International Exhibition of the Decorative Arts, called for the razing of some of the oldest and most densely populated sectors of Paris in the second, third, ninth, and tenth arrondissements (districts). This caused an uproar among the Parisian administrators who, by the turn of the twentieth century, had come to see the city's center as inviolable—an ironic stance, given that Haussmann himself had bulldozed his way through its very center decades earlier. Le Corbusier proposed cruciform skyscrapers to get urban density under control and also sought to introduce integrated green spaces and nature into such configurations. A devotee of the straight line ("man walks in a straight line because he has a goal"), he embraced the importance of speed in the modern city.

Le Corbusier embraced speed in relation to contemporary transport and envisioned improved traffic flows as a critical part of his urban reconfiguration. In fact, the patron of his controversial 1925 plan, Gabriel Voisin, was a major pioneer in aviation, having created the first heavier-than-air, engine-powered, controlled flying machine. The designer of many military planes, he had by the 1920s moved on to automobiles he called Avions (airplanes) Voisin, which were known for their use of light materials and aerodynamic design.

Over the course of the twentieth century, from the building of La Défense (the urban industrial park west of the city limits) between 1958 and the 1970s to projects such as the Tour Montparnasse skyscraper in the southern central part of town, Paris planners would not embrace vertical building within the city itself. Nonetheless, machine aesthetics and a dedication to the new building materials dominated rebuilding in twentieth century Paris. Critics have regarded such buildings as the Pompidou Center, in the heart of the district Le Corbusier envisaged for the Voisin Plan, as evidence of taking the building-as-machine too literally. The most recent systematic renovation of the capital under François Mitterrand consisted of glass and steel architecture in new buildings for important institutions such as the National Library and the Opéra, a new arch at La Défense, and the I. M. Pei–designed glass pyramid at the Louvre. This building project can be seen as part of a long tradition of changes that are not rejections of industrialization but rather embody the popularization of the idea that technical mastery should take aestheticized form.

Transportation

In France as well as in other Western countries, transportation has played an equally important role in moving toward the future in both time and space. Since the nineteenth century, mechanized transportation was not simply redefining cities but also the relation of city to country, and between countries and other parts of the world. If trade, technology, transportation, and travel can be thought to have shaped the modern world in general, France has been a major part of contributing to such global transformations and has been transformed by them. While the migration of people across national boundaries and borders has often posed a challenge to definitions of French identity, mobility has also facilitated tourism and travel to France—and these have crystallized a vision of Frenchness for foreigners and to the French through this foreign gaze. Underlying the expansion of tourism, a worldwide network of

10. The building's infrastructure is on the outside of the Pompidou Center, Paris's modern art museum. Richard Rogers and Renzo Piano's 1970s futuristic design showed an appreciation for technology and infrastructure as integral to notions of modernity, even in art.

transportation infrastructure and vehicles, powered first by steam and then by electricity and oil, all reliant on technological mastery, have made moving possible and even pleasurable.

The transportation revolution was not explicitly or primarily French, but France, England, Germany, the United States, Italy, and eventually Japan have all been created anew by the embrace of these changes. In addition, these technological changes remade much of the world with the export of such things as trains (the French built the railways in Russia, for example) and cars to nonproducing nations. That said, Ernest Michaux invented the modern pedal bicycle in 1861, and by 1914 there were 3.5 million bicycles in France alone. French car production was second only to America's and such firms as Renault, Peugeot, and Citroën early on mastered mass-produced stylishness. At the same time, Michelin, supplied by the rich resource of rubber plants in French Indochina, competed only with the British company Dunlop for worldwide tire dominance, having innovated the removable pneumatic tire.

Even before industrialization, the French were the first to undertake large-scale canal construction (begun in 1604 and completed in 1642, when the Briare Canal joined the Loire and the Seine Rivers). French canal-building took on global significance and made enormous profits when Ferdinand de Lesseps secured the rights in the 1850s from Said Pasha, the viceroy of Egypt, to build a canal that would cut the distance from London to Bombay by half. When he had visited Egypt, Prosper Enfantin, the Saint-Simonian who led a sect to settle in Egypt, surmised that the Red Sea and the Mediterranean were at the same level and believed that only political as opposed to technological barriers existed to the building of a canal to join them. Funded by French investors and designed by an Austrian engineer, the canal was opened to boats of all nations, but overwhelmingly traveled by the British. Thus, the Suez Canal was truly an international affair in its design and use when it was inaugurated in 1869 in the presence of many European heads of state and royals. The inauguration was actually presided over by Empress Eugénie of France, suggesting the way that France took the lead in this international commercial order.

The Suez Canal served not only as a major commercial route but also, along with the opening of the American transcontinental railway, made circumnavigating the globe remarkably faster—two achievements that are, not coincidentally, key facts of the story of *Around the World in Eighty Days* (1872). Later in the century, one could perhaps say that the spectacular French failure in the construction of the Panama Canal (the French erred in trying to dig at sea-level, and the workers died in droves from malaria and yellow fever) was a sign of the fragility of France's leading role in technological fields. The outcome can even be understood as particularly prescient regarding the future of foreign affairs since the Americans ended up completing the lock-and-dam canal there twenty years later (when the mosquito-driven cause of malaria was also understood).

Although trains were originally an appendage of mining (tracks were laid and carts hauled coal), the British built the first autonomous route between Liverpool and Manchester in 1830 as steam pumps and steam engines, fed by coal (and thus by human labor rather than nature's wind and water) sped up life in Europe. It may be disputable whether department stores or train stations became the cathedrals of the nineteenth century, but it is fair to say that without the trains, there would be no department stores. Trains created enormous internal migration throughout Europe, increasing the population in cities, which then supported the growth of consumer culture. They made the supply of goods more plentiful, hauling both passengers and cargo from the periphery to the center. Marx envisioned the train as a political liberator that would serve as the hearse carrying feudalism and absolutism to their graves. While perhaps a tad optimistic, especially given the role trains came to play in supplying arms and leading civilians en masse to their deaths in both world wars, the enthusiasm evinced by Marx for newfangled transport technologies has seen a particular expression in France, where, perhaps emerging from their utopianism, France has clearly displayed a mastery of the "very high" tech in transportation.

While it may seem quaint today, the Montgolfier hot-air balloon stunned those in 1783 who had not thought it possible to breathe up in the sky. The Marquis d'Arlandes and the scientist Jean-François Pîlatre de Rozier proved them wrong while also showing the French panache for science and flight. As was the case with the cinema, aviation innovations and pioneers in France and America exchanged information and competed in ways that made it overdetermined that Gaumont and Pathé would establish production in America as well as in France, and that Henry Farman, inventor of the biplane, and Gabriel Voisin would compete with Wilbur and Orville Wright. Louis Blériot crossed the English Channel in an airplane only eight months after the Wright brothers had managed to fly higher than 100 meters. With this intense connection between France and America in the history of aviation, it should come as no surprise that Charles Lindbergh would go out of his way to land in Paris during his 1927 transatlantic flight.

Aside from the key role France played in the early history of aviation, France continued to innovate in both military and civil aviation over the course of the twentieth century. Wartime aeronautics in the nineteenth century included sixty-five manned balloons, 381 pigeons, five dogs, eleven tons of dispatches, and 2.5 million letters transported during the siege of Paris in the Franco-Prussian war. The French military uses of airspace have continued apace. The Dassault Company developed the Mirage fighters, which are among the most globally supplied planes of its kind. During the 1960s and on the heels of the Soviet Sputnik launch, the French inserted themselves as a third competitor in the space race, beyond the Cold War powers of the USSR and the United States. They became the third nation to launch its own satellite (Astérix One) from a French space booster called the Diamant.

The strength of French aviation can also be seen in the early and successful creation of the Caravelle jet plane by Sud Aviation. Flown in 1959, it was one of the first well-functioning jets made for commercial use. (The British de Havilland Comet had serious technical failings despite its earlier appearance.) With design innovations that put the jets behind the wings and provided a much quieter ride, the Caravelle also changed aviation history when United Airlines purchased twenty of the French-made planes, internationalizing the suppliers of planes to U.S. carriers, which until then had been supplied only by American companies.

The success of the Caravelle also paved the way for thinking that France could indeed compete with the United States. This led to the creation of the sexiest of high-speed futuristic air projects: the Concorde.

Now that the Concorde no longer flies, its history has been recast mostly as a project about the folly of the leading edge of high-tech fields mixing with high-stakes politics. But the Concorde's history helps us understand the way that France accrued national prestige while managing to build transnational partnerships in high-tech fields such as aviation. Since the 1990s, France has played a defining role in Airbus, an international partnership whose headquarters are in Toulouse, France.

It is fair to say that the initial enthusiasm for the Concorde included a bid at surpassing the Americans in technological supremacy, but it can also be seen as part of the French tradition of dreaming up highly futuristic technological possibilities. Although retrospectively it is thought that the British and the French, who undertook the project jointly, never really could work together (including a dispute over the "e" at the end, which led the British to call it "Concorde," dropping the French use of the article before the noun), the realities of the Concorde's limitations were its expense per passenger. The plane debuted more or less at the same time as the world's largest passenger plane, the Boeing 747, during the energy crisis of the 1970s. The Concorde's speed (whose supersonic duration was limited to the over-the-water period because of the environmental concerns about sonic boom) came at great expense: the plane used as much fuel as a B-747 but carried only one-fourth the number of passengers. In addition, it required more than the usual number of hours on the ground for maintenance. The Concorde seemed a frivolous and beautiful toy of the super-wealthy. It is not clear that jets actually needed to go that fast, but the achievement was nevertheless both a boon to the French aviation industry and a lesson: France would thereafter commit to making planes that would sell, and the Airbus program has proven they could.

Not only is France particularly high-tech, but after World War II the notion of "dirigisme"—an active policy of state interventionism in the guidance and management of technology—has facilitated its development at the leading edge, enhanced by large state programs that fund research, development, and application. When de Gaulle came to power (both times), it became his goal to achieve French greatness through technology. After the saga of defeat and collaboration in World War II, the French government sought international recognition and its own sense of security and autonomy in the realm of high tech. The period from 1945 to 1975 witnessed the tripling of purchasing power. The GNP grew at 5.5 percent a year as France took up nuclear power with gusto, advanced in aviation, outer space, and computer technology. Technology functioned not just to maintain economic and military independence; it also linked France internally and internationally, since technology's complexity and its underlying drive demanded greater connection in time and space

The story of the TGV (Train à Grand Vitesse) suggests that France could be at the cutting edge of technology and still provide mass transport, at least within the borders of the nation since the TGV project initially stopped at France's frontiers. During the postwar period, France committed to developing high-speed train travel. Concerned about losing riders to air transport and aware of the Japanese success with the Shinkansen (bullet) train, the government-owned SNCF (the result of the nationalization of the five main railway lines in 1938) in cooperation with the French multinational power corporation, Alstom, developed a fast and sleek train that was put into service between Paris and Lyon in 1982. It used existing rails and was powered by electricity rather than gas turbines. New design for the sharing of wheel trucks with adjacent cars allowed the design of a lighter and more rigid body, creating a simultaneously sexy and cost-effective train. As a result, the train could provide the new service at affordable prices, underscored by the slogan for the new train, "Progress means nothing unless it is shared by all." This high-speed train technology has been a backbone of European integration.

Communication and information

A more interesting case of the peculiarity of the French mobilization of nationally based technological sophistication can be grasped in the story of the success of the Minitel. Born from the idea that information itself could be rationalized and computerized even before the Internet existed, the Minitel is a telephone-based network using the closed system of the French phone company, France Telecom. The initial motivation came from the will to save the government-owned phone company the expense of printing directories. Since its introduction in 1984, the Minitel's more than 17 million users (one in four French households and about one-third of the adult population) define a delimited group of users in an electronic version of French community. Still used to access bank accounts, conduct e-commerce, and make travel reservations, before 1997 it generated more trade inside France than the Internet attracted worldwide.

Although there are many ways to interpret its success (and its persistence despite the Internet) the French government's commitment to the project and the simplicity of its kiosk billing system made it both cheap and easy to use. Customers were offered a free terminal in the place of receiving the traditional telephone book. Just as Amazon.com has underwritten the cost of e-books, France Telecom subsidized the system until it broke even because they wanted it to be adopted. Aside from information, the system provided communication. Users connected to each other (a system of proto-email), and this gave rise to the birth of the "Minitel rose," online sex chatting, suggesting the intersection of both commercial and personal interests in the system. When it launched its Wanadoo Internet service, France Telecom thought it would phase out the Minitel, a slower service through which people were paying for information they could now get for free, but users protested and the phone company currently maintains both systems. For some in France, the Internet is an American version of the Minitel, and French voices have been among those raised the loudest about the cultural and linguistic Anglophone imperialism of cyberspace. This concern has also resulted in a commitment to the digitization of books in languages other than English, led by Jean-Noël Jeanneney, former head of the French National Library.

If France has its technological dreamers, it also has had its fair share of clever critics. Jacques Tati is now fondly remembered for the films he made in the late 1950s and '60s that are wry critiques of the conformity and the self-indulgence of high-tech living. In *Mon Oncle*, a parvenu plastics manufacturer and his family live in a high-tech household, complete with automatic doors, an electric kitchen that Tati cannot figure out how to work, and a pretentious newfangled metal fountain shaped like a fish that sent water spouting from its mouth. *Playtime* begins with aerial views of the clouds descending into an antiseptic, all-metal airport represented as the new town square worthy of spoofing, before the film moves on to apartment buildings and visions of the organization of residential and commercial space—right out of Le Corbusier. What was once the future has arrived, and Tati's films ask the viewer to consider such blind utopianism with a skeptical eye. Although Tati's films have stood in for the French critique of the technological society, the fact that they spoof France for its earnest embrace of household gadgets, modern living, car mania and the love of high-speed transportation suggests that the society was obviously deeply implicated in technophilia in the first place; otherwise the jokes would not be funny.

Since the Enlightenment, French belief in progress and the nation's investment in the future has sometimes developed at a pace that can best be described as "hurtling into the future." The high-tech solution has been often imagined and envisioned, and sometimes well executed, as in the TGV. In this way, France has played a key role in the development of what we might call Western technological modernity. Its French "paradox" may be that it has managed to embrace the future without erasing its past. Where else do we find such juxtaposition and even contradiction as the I. M. Pei pyramid at the Louvre? On its 120th anniversary, the Eiffel Tower was lighted to look as if it were dancing—still beautiful and optimistic, after all these years.

Conclusion

When the Eiffel Tower opened in 1889, the statesman-turned-journalist Jules Simon declared, "We are all citizens of the Eiffel Tower." This universalist vision of the Republic at its centennial sheds light on the choice of Jessye Norman, an African American woman draped in a French flag singing the national anthem, for the French bicentennial celebration in 1989. The notion that a thousand-foot tower located in Paris belonged to the world is consistent with the modern government vision of France and its role as a place in and for the rest of the world. Yet a government's symbolic gestures crafted for large audiences can also regrettably flatten the diversity of experiences on the ground that make up a nation's and a people's history as well as the complex alchemy out of which nations and peoples continue to be formed.

The realities of modern France are far more multifaceted than the visions proffered through such public spectacles of nationalism, as this short introduction hopes to have shown. In the world today, power redounds to those able to draw diverse peoples together in and across place, rather than one in which physical distance is used as a basis for maintaining power, especially over far-flung empires. Because France is, and has been, a literal crossroads, it is even more worthy of consideration. Not only have the actions of people in France contributed to the present global condition, but

French people have also invoked the human and universal in ways that go beyond using it as an excuse for imperial conquest. France thus offers a bright mirror in which we can see as many triumphs as tragedies over the course of the last two hundred years. The Revolution's world spirit shaped it as a global event, and subsequent democratic movements have modeled their own aspirations in a knowing relation to what happened in France in 1789.

There is no point in looking at France through rose-tinted glasses, nor in bemoaning or celebrating its decline. New ways of examining the past from our contemporary context have resulted in rethinking the coherence of place, especially the usual focus on the nation as the central object of history. We now have a new appreciation of diasporic cultures, of migrations, rootlessness, borderlands, the transnational mixing of cultures and identities, and for the images and objects that speed across cultures and through space. Yet all these formulations make France more important, not less so. Things that happened in the place of France and in its name also shed significant light on these very issues of place and mobility in the contemporary world.

This new way of thinking about the past also makes French history new again. Few national cultures have engaged with considerations of citizenship in such global terms; few have articulated the value of linguistic and literary traditions, been shaped by their interaction in the world, cultivated the power of a great capital as a world crossroads, grappled with the challenges of cultural diversity and the role of ethnic and religious identity in reshaping national culture, and embraced the centrality of technology in fostering global communication and determining the shape of the global future as has France. We can look both at France as well as to France for insights into the simultaneously rapid integration of cultures and the concomitant proliferation of differences that characterize the modern world.

We cannot easily resolve the complex and seemingly contradictory conditions of the present global experience. If France has taught us anything, it is that sometimes living with contradiction is a necessary and even wise course of action. Josephine Baker, herself an African American transplant, expressed this typically French duality in the 1930s, in one of the most famous French songs of the twentieth century: "I have two loves," sang Baker, "My country and Paris....My savannah is beautiful, but what good does it do to deny it: What seduces me is Paris, all of Paris....To see it one day is my beautiful dream." For Baker as for other global citizens, Paris, like all of France, lives on as a geographical crossroads, a seductive ideal, and a dream of the future.

References

Introduction

Ernest Lavisse, "France, since the Revolution," in *Realms of Memory*, ed. Pierre Nora, Lawrence D. Kritzman, and Arthur Goldhammer (New York: Columbia University Press, 1997), 183.

Chapter 1

Montmorency, quoted in Lynn Hunt, *The French Revolution and Human Rights: A Brief Documentary History*, illus. ed. (Boston: Bedford, 1996), 73.

Tonnere, in Hunt, *French Revolution and Human Rights*, 86.

Lavisse, "We believed," quoted in Pierre Nora, Lawrence D. Kritzman, and Arthur Goldhammer, *Realms of Memory* (New York: Columbia University Press, 1997), 154.

Lavisse, "You should love France," quoted in Nora et al., *Realms of Memory*, 169.

Vidal de la Blache, quoted in Nora et al., 188.

Jules Michelet, quoted in Nora et al., 192.

Charles de Gaulle, "Providence has created," from *The Complete War Memoirs of Charles de Gaulle* (New York: Carroll and Graf, 1998), 3.

Nicolas Sarkozy, quoted in Steven Englund, "More like the Anglo-Saxons," *Commonweal*, June 15, 2007.

Chapter 2

Malraux, in Herman Lebovics, *Mona Lisa's Escort: André Malraux and the Reinvention of French Culture* (Ithaca, NY: Cornell University Press, 1999), 89.

Malraux on de Gaulle, in Lawrence D. Kritzman, "A Certain Idea of de Gaulle," *Yale French Studies* 111, 157–68; see also special issue *Myth and Modernity* (2007): 166–67.

Jaurès, "Our Colonies," cited in Dennis Ager, *Identity, Insecurity and Image: France and Language* (Clevedon, England: Multilingual Matters, 1999), 238.

Chapter 3

Queen Victoria, "Everything is so truly regal," in Alistair Horne, *La Belle France: A Short History* (New York: Vintage Books, 2006), 262.

Jacques Chirac, "By choosing the Louvre," from "Louvre Abu Dhabi to be created within the Saadiyat Island Cultural District," *Al Bawaba* http://www1.albawaba.com/en/business/louvre-abu-dhabi-be-created-within-saadiyat-island-cultural-district; accessed November 11, 2010.

Stein, "Paris was where…" from *The Making of Americans (1934)*, cited in J. Gerald Kennedy, *Imagining Paris: Exile, Writing, and American Identity* (New Haven, CT: Yale University Press, 1993), 43.

Henri Michaux, "Lieux lointains," *Mercure de France*, no. 1109 (1 January 1956) as cited in Pascale Casanova, translated by M. B. DeBevoise, *The World Republic of Letters* (Cambridge, MA: Harvard University Press, 2004), 2.

Chapter 4

On information about racial laws see "Vichy Discrimination against Jews in North Africa," http://www.ushmm.org/wlc/en/article.php?ModuleId=10007311, accessed November 11, 2010.

For some of the statistics cited on immigration, see Patrick Weil, "Bringing in the Banlieues," *American Interest* 4, no. 4 (Spring 2009), http://www.the-american-interest.com/article.cfm?piece=564.

Conclusion

Jules Simon on the Eiffel Tower, quoted in Charles Braibant, *Histoire de la Tour Eiffel* (Paris: Plon, 1964).

Further reading

General

Gildea, Robert. *France since 1945*. Oxford: Oxford University Press, 1996.

Horne, Alistair. *La Belle France: A Short History*. New York: Vintage Books, 2006.

Kedward, Rod. *La Vie en bleu: France and the French Since 1900*. London: Penguin Books, 2006.

Mollier, Jean-Yves, and Jocelyn Georges. *La Plus longue des Républiques: 1870–1940*. Paris: Fayard, 1994.

Moynahan, Brian. *The French Century: An Illustrated History of Modern France*. Paris: Flammarion; distributed in North America by Rizzoli International, 2007.

Popkin, Jeremy D. *A History of Modern France*. 3rd ed. Upper Saddle River, NJ: Pearson/Prentice Hall, 2005.

Zeldin, Theodore. *France, 1848–1945*. 2 vols. Oxford: Clarendon Press, 1973–77.

Chapter 1

Bell, David A. *The Cult of the Nation in France: Inventing Nationalism, 1680–1800*. Cambridge, MA: Harvard University Press, 2003.

———. *The First Total War: Napoleon's Europe and the Birth of Warfare as We Know It*. Boston: Mariner Books, Houghton Mifflin Harcourt, 2008.

Doyle, William. *The French Revolution: A Very Short Introduction.*
New York: Oxford University Press, 2001.

Fritzsche, Peter. *Stranded in the Present: Modern Time and the
Melancholy of History.* Cambridge, MA: Harvard University Press,
2004).

Furet, François, and Mona Ozouf. *A Critical Dictionary of the French
Revolution.* 1st ed. Cambridge, MA: Belknap Press of Harvard
University Press, 1989.

Gerson, Stéphane. *The Pride of Place: Local Memories and Political
Culture in Nineteenth-Century France.* Ithaca, NY: Cornell
University Press, 2003.

Hunt, Lynn. *Politics, Culture, and Class in the French Revolution.*
20th anniversary ed. Berkeley: University of California Press,
2004.

———. *The French Revolution and Human Rights: A Brief
Documentary History.* Illustrated ed. Boston: Bedford, 1996.

Marx, Karl. *The Eighteenth Brumaire of Louis Bonaparte.* Translated
by D. D. L. New York: Mondial, 2005.

Nora, Pierre, Lawrence D. Kritzman, and Arthur Goldhammer.
Realms of Memory. New York: Columbia University Press, 1997.

Ozouf, Mona. *Festivals and the French Revolution.* Cambridge, MA:
Harvard University Press, 1991.

Tocqueville, Alexis de. *The Old Régime and the French Revolution.* 1st
Anchor Books ed. New York: Anchor Books, 1983.

Weber, Eugen. *Peasants into Frenchmen: The Modernization of Rural
France, 1870–1914.* 1st ed. Stanford, CA: Stanford University Press,
1976.

Wilder, Gary. *The French Imperial Nation-State: Negritude and
Colonial Humanism between the Two World Wars.* 1st ed. Chicago:
University of Chicago Press, 2005.

Chapter 2

Ager, Dennis. *Identity, Insecurity and Image: France and Language.*
Clevedon, UK: Multilingual Matters, 1999.

Bredin, Jean-Denis. *The Affair: The Case of Alfred Dreyfus.* New York:
G. Braziller, 1986.

Burns, Michael. *France and the Dreyfus Affair: A Documentary
History.* Illus. ed. Boston: Bedford/St. Martin's, 1999.

Chaplin, Tamara. *Turning On the Mind: French Philosophers on
Television.* Chicago: University of Chicago Press, 2007.

Conklin, Alice. *A Mission to Civilize: The Republican Idea of Empire in France and West Africa, 1895–1930*. 1st ed. Stanford, CA.: Stanford University Press, 1997.

Cusset, François. *French Theory: How Foucault, Derrida, Deleuze, and Co. Transformed the Intellectual Life of the United States*. Minneapolis: University of Minnesota Press, 2008.

Daughton, J. P. *An Empire Divided: Religion, Republicanism, and the Making of French Colonialism, 1880–1914*. New York: Oxford University Press, 2008.

Kaplan, Alice Yaeger. *French Lessons: A Memoir*. 4th ed. Chicago: University of Chicago Press, 1994.

Lebovics, Herman. *Mona Lisa's Escort: André Malraux and the Reinvention of French Culture*. Ithaca, NY: Cornell University Press, 1999.

Loyer, Emanuelle. "Les Intellectuelles et la television." In *La Grande Aventure du petit écran: La Télévision française, 1935–75*, edited by Jérome Bourdon et al., 80–83. Nanterre: Musée d'histoire contemporaine-BDIC, 1997.

Nadeau, Jean-Benoît, and Julie Barlow. *The Story of French*. London: Portico, 2008.

Reid, Donald. "The Role of the Intellectual." In *The Transformation of Modern France: Essays in Honor of Gordon Wright*, edited by William B. Cohen, 109–24. Boston: Houghton Mifflin, 1997.

Rodrigue, Aron. *French Jews, Turkish Jews: The Alliance Israélite Universelle and the Politics of Jewish Schooling in Turkey, 1860–1925*. Bloomington: Indiana University Press, 1990.

Roger, Philippe. *The American Enemy: The History of French Anti-Americanism*. Chicago: University of Chicago Press, 2006.

Chapter 3

Benjamin, Walter. *The Arcades Project*. Cambridge, MA: Belknap Press of Harvard University Press, 2002.

Casanova, Pascale. *The World Republic of Letters*. Translated by M. B. DeBevoise. Cambridge, MA: Harvard University Press, 2004.

Edwards, Brent Hayes. *The Practice of Diaspora: Literature, Translation, and the Rise of Black Internationalism*. Cambridge, MA: Harvard University Press, 2003.

Endy, Christopher. *Cold War Holidays: American Tourism in France*. Chapel Hill: University of North Carolina Press, 2004.

Higonnet, Patrice L. R. *Paris: Capital of the World*. Cambridge, MA: Belknap Press of Harvard University Press, 2005.

Levenstein, Harvey A. *We'll Always Have Paris: American Tourists in France since 1930*. Chicago: University of Chicago Press, 2004.

Nord, Philip G. *Impressionists and Politics: Art and Democracy in the Nineteenth Century*. London: Routledge, 2000.

Schwartz, Vanessa R. *Spectacular Realities: Early Mass Culture in Fin-de-Siècle Paris*. Berkeley: University of California Press, 1998.

Silverman, Debora L. *Art Nouveau in Fin-de-Siècle France: Politics, Psychology, and Style*. Berkeley: University of California Press, 1989.

Spang, Rebecca L. *The Invention of the Restaurant: Paris and Modern Gastronomic Culture*. Cambridge, MA: Harvard University Press, 2001.

Stovall, Tyler Edward. *Paris Noir: African Americans in the City of Light*. Boston: Houghton Mifflin, 1996.

Troy, Nancy J. *Couture Culture: A Study in Modern Art and Fashion*. Cambridge, MA: MIT Press, 2003.

Chapter 4

Amara, Fadela, and Sylvia Zappi. *Breaking the Silence: French Women's Voices from the Ghetto*. 1st ed. Berkeley: University of California Press, 2006.

Bancel, Nicolas, Pascal Blanchard, and Françoise Vergès. *La Colonisation française*. Toulouse: Milan, 2007.

Bell, David A. "Trapped by History: France and Its Jews." *World Affairs* 172, no. 1 (Summer 2009): 24–34.

Bowen, John Richard. *Why the French Don't Like Headscarves: Islam, the State and Public Space*. Princeton, NJ: Princeton University Press, 2007.

Caldwell, Christopher. *Reflections on the Revolution in Europe: Immigration, Islam, and the West*. New York: Doubleday, 2009.

Dubois, Laurent. *A Colony of Citizens: Revolution and Slave Emancipation in the French Caribbean, 1787–1804*. Chapel Hill: For the Omohundro Institute of Early American History and Culture, Williamsburg, VA, by the University of North Carolina Press, 2004.

Giry, Stéphane. "France and Its Muslims." *Foreign Affairs* 85, no. 5 (September–October 2006): 87–104.

Gresh, Alain. *L'Islam, la République et le monde*. Paris: Fayard, 2004.

Jeuland, Yves. "Comme un juif en France." Documentary film. Paris: Editions France Télévisions Distribution, 2007.

Lorcin, Patricia M. E. *Imperial Identities: Stereotyping, Prejudice and Race in Colonial Algeria.* London: I. B. Tauris, 1999.

Marrus, Michael Robert, and Robert O. Paxton. *Vichy France and the Jews: With a New Foreword [1995] by Stanley Hoffmann.* Stanford, CA: Stanford University Press, 1995.

Noiriel, Gérard. *The French Melting Pot: Immigration, Citizenship, and National Identity.* Minneapolis: University of Minnesota Press, 1996.

Rosenberg, Clifford D. *Policing Paris: The Origins of Modern Immigration Control Between the Wars.* Ithaca, NY: Cornell University Press, 2006.

Scott, Joan Wallach. *The Politics of the Veil.* Princeton, NJ: Princeton University Press, 2007.

Shepard, Todd. *The Invention of Decolonization: The Algerian War and the Remaking of France.* 2nd ed. Ithaca, NY: Cornell University Press, 2008.

Témime, Emile. *France, terre d'immigration.* Paris: Gallimard, 1999.

Weil, Patrick. "Bringing in the Banlieues." *American Interest* 4, no. 4 (Spring 2009): 62–68.

——— . *How to Be French: Nationality in the Making since 1789.* Durham, NC: Duke University Press, 2009.

Chapter 5

Alder, Ken. *Engineering the Revolution: Arms and Enlightenment, 1763–1815.* Princeton, NJ: Princeton University Press, 1999.

Bess, Michael. *The Light-Green Society: Ecology and Technological Modernity in France, 1960–2000.* Chicago: University of Chicago Press, 2003.

Busbea, Larry. *Topologies: The Urban Utopia in France, 1960–1970.* Cambridge, MA: MIT Press, 2007.

Castells, Manuel. *The Information Age: Economy, Society, and Culture.* 2nd ed. Cambridge, MA: Blackwell, 2000.

Chadeau, Emmanuel. *Le Rêve et la puissance, l'avion et son siècle.* Paris: Fayard, 1996.

Chapman, Herrick. *State Capitalism and Working-Class Radicalism in the French Aircraft Industry.* Berkeley: University of California Press, 1990.

Cohen, Jean-Louis. *Le Corbusier, 1887–1965: The Lyricism of Architecture in the Machine Age*. Köln: Taschen, 2005.

———. *Scenes of the World to Come: European Architecture and the American Challenge, 1893–1960*. English ed. Paris: Flammarion and Montréal: Canadian Center for Architecture, 1995.

Darnton, Robert. *The Business of Enlightenment: A Publishing History of the* Encyclopédie, *1775–1800*. Cambridge, MA: Belknap Press of Harvard University Press, 1979.

Fierro, Annette. *The Glass State: The Technology of the Spectacle, Paris, 1981–1998*. Cambridge, MA: MIT Press, 2006.

Guigueno, Vincent. "Building a High-Speed Society: France and the Aérotrain, 1962–1974." *Technology and Culture* 49, no. 1 (January 2008): 21–40.

Hecht, Gabrielle. *The Radiance of France: Nuclear Power and National Identity after World War II*. Cambridge, MA: MIT Press, 1998.

Levin, Miriam R. *When the Eiffel Tower Was New: French Visions of Progress at the Centennial of the Revolution*. South Hadley, MA: Mount Holyoke College Art Museum; distributed by University of Massachusetts Press, Amherst, 1989.

Panchasi, Roxanne. *Future Tense: The Culture of Anticipation in France Between the Wars*. Ithaca, NY: Cornell University Press, 2009.

Picon, Antoine. *Les Saint-simoniens: Raison, imaginaire et utopie*. Paris: Belin, 2002.

Picon-Lefèbvre, Virginie. *Paris—Ville moderne: Maine-Montparnasse et La Défense, 1950–1975*. Paris: Norma Editions, 2003.

Syon, Guillaume de. "Consuming Concorde." *Technology and Culture* 44, no. 3 (July 2003): 650–54.

Verne, Jules. *Around the World in Eighty Days*. London and New York: Penguin Classics, 2004.

Wakeman, Rosemary. *Modernizing the Provincial City: Toulouse 1945–1975*. Cambridge, MA: Harvard University Press, 1997.

Williams, Rosalind H. *Notes on the Underground: An Essay on Technology, Society, and the Imagination*. Cambridge, MA: MIT Press, 1992.

Modern France

Index

Index

Modern France